MARIANNE CHRISTIAN
BURKHALTER + SUMI

MARIANNE   CHRISTIAN

BURKHALTER + SUMI

PHOTOS BY HEINRICH HELFENSTEIN

TEXTS BY LYNNETTE WIDDER, STEVEN SPIER,

EUGENE ASSE AND DETLEF MERTINS

PRINCETON ARCHITECTURAL PRESS · NEW YORK

PUBLIC BUILDINGS – SPACE AND THE PUBLIC

LYNNETTE WIDDER

Zurich does largely without formal spaces of public appearance.[1] One exception to this rule is the convergence at the city's center of two large-scale urban vistas: from the quay in front of the main train station up towards the domed central buildings of the University (1914, by Karl Moser) and Federal Polytechnic Institute (ETH) (1863, by Gottfried Semper; dome addition 1923 by Gustav Gull) on the opposite hillside; and from the terrace behind the ETH, which overlooks the Limmat River. In a city characterized by agglomerative, topographically stratified structures at its center, and boulevards largely unmodulated by points de vues along its Gründerzeit edges, the distance afforded by these two vistas allows the recipient to position himself vis-à-vis the city, laid out in its panoramic entirety. At the same time, it constructs the dominant moments in the urban landscape around the two educational institutions. The way in which public space is represented by these examples of urbanism in its nineteenth-century sense is still relevant to architectural culture: their public status derives from their reception at a distance by a contemplative viewing subject, and from their ability to communicate social significance through architecture. The space inside the ETH's dome is the site of one of Marianne Burkhalter and Christian Sumi's more recent projects. Its

---

[1] The definition of the "space of public appearance" as an architecture which could "not only house the public realm, but also represent its reality" derives from Kenneth Frampton's reading of Hannah Arendt's *The Human Condition*. See "Modern Architecture and the Critical Present," *Architectural Design* 7–8 (1982): 7–20.

public status, too, derives from its amenability to contemplative reception of its forms, and from its evocation of culturally relevant associations in order to communicate meaning.

Marianne Burkhalter and Christian Sumi were commissioned to install a virtual reality projection theater in the dome while maintaining existing workstations along its periphery. The installation – a wafer-thin, curved, self-supporting screen framed by a luxuriant curtain – is reduced in its form to a primary geometry, a circle segment. By reasserting the contours of the dome by means of indirect lighting and by the removal of heavy ancillary structures dating from the 70s, the architects have allowed the form of the space to reassert itself; spatial legibility in turn evokes associations with the dome as a type.

At the same time, the installation is richly associative, although it foregoes any iconographic reference to the advanced technology it accommodates. The associations which the visitor may have are directly related to his role within the space. For the member of the audience who encounters the curved screen frontally upon entrance, it is a proscenium. Seen from the mezzanine, where the students who gather informally around the balustrade during projections comprise a kind of unofficial upper tier, it is an anatomical theater. The suspended ring along which the curtain slides reiterates the dome's center; the installation's series of concentric forms restates the perimeter geometry. As the curtains are drawn together around audience and screen, rather than drawn apart to reveal the screen, as in the cinema, the proscenium becomes an amphitheater. The dimming of the general lighting and the illumination at the dome's apogee of a blue neon ring – itself as evocative of commercial signage as of Dan Flavin's work – heighten the sense of the event and the explicitness of the dome's geometric recession. The architecture's formal specificity is inextricable from the event it raises to the level of public significance.

Consider a slightly earlier project, the Business School in Laufenburg. The school stands on a street, lined in gap-tooth fashion with modest two-story buildings and which continues on uninterruptedly past the school, precluding the possibility of a distanced, frontal viewpoint. Façade elements – wooden cladding, fenestration, roof details – consequently wrap the building's corners, so that the façades recompose themselves in different configurations as the approaching visitor's oblique angle of vision shifts. At the same time, the elements themselves retain the greatest possible scalar and semantic ambivalence: the unmullioned front window is as big as the entry wind-break, while the actual door is almost concealed. The wood cladding is completely reticent about floor-to-floor heights or sectional relationships. Because nothing is identifiable according to relative size or conventional expression of function, the composition of three sloped volumes attains a degree of abstraction which focuses the recipient's attention on its prismatic qualities.

On entry, the visitor is finally afforded an overview of the building's inner life. Only when seen from the entry hall does the school's split section allow for a view up and down into the broad hallways joining classrooms, as well as through glazing into the computer labs and library. The continuity of view through the building gathers communal activity along lines

16 ▶

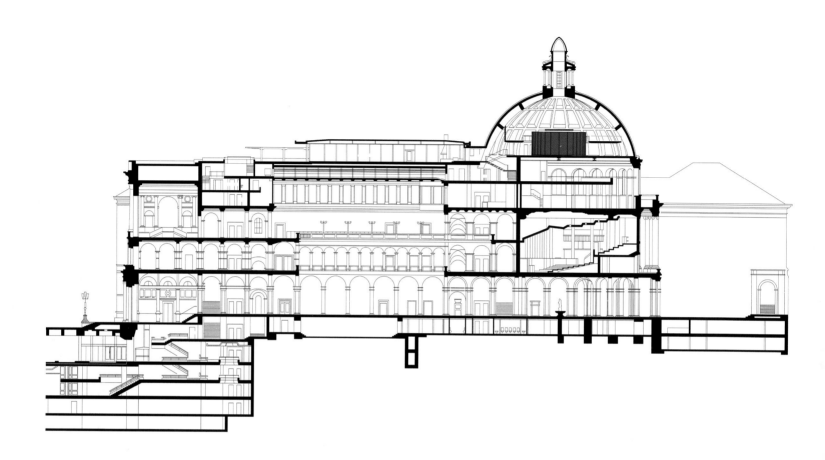

DOME INTERIOR/VISUALIZATION CENTER, ETH ZURICH, 1997

Client: Amt für Bundesbauten, 4th District, Zurich ▌ Collaborators: Hermann Kohler, Angelika Crola ▌ Project architects: WAP Architekten AG,

Zurich ▌ Engineer: Stucki Hofacker + Partner AG, Zurich ▌ Lighting Planning: Christian Vogt, Ingenieurbüro für Lichttechnik, Winterthur

In the "VisDome," the visualization centers of the various ETH departments (architecture, systems engineering, chemistry, geology, etc.) are united in a single, greater institute. The project intentionally refrains from staging every high-tech appliance, as is often the case at trade fairs, but attempts instead to create a space or environment for the "virtual image" – particularly given the incredible architectural density that already exists in the head zone of the ETH building. The core of the complex is formed by the new curved screen, nine meters in diameter, which generates a series of additional constructive measures – beamer-ring, red curtain, black linoleum floor covering, etc. – that add to the spatial exaggeration of the 1923 dome by Gull. The spatial installation during the Exposition de la Mode by Lilly Reich and Mies van der Rohe (1927) was an important reference for us with regard to the use of textiles for structuring space.

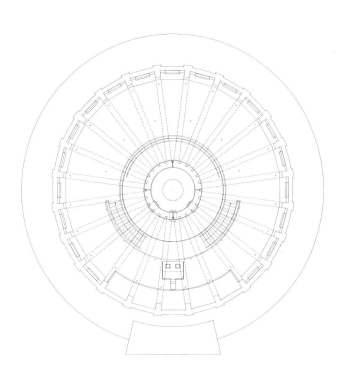

Ground plan ▮ Interior of dome with screen and beamer ring

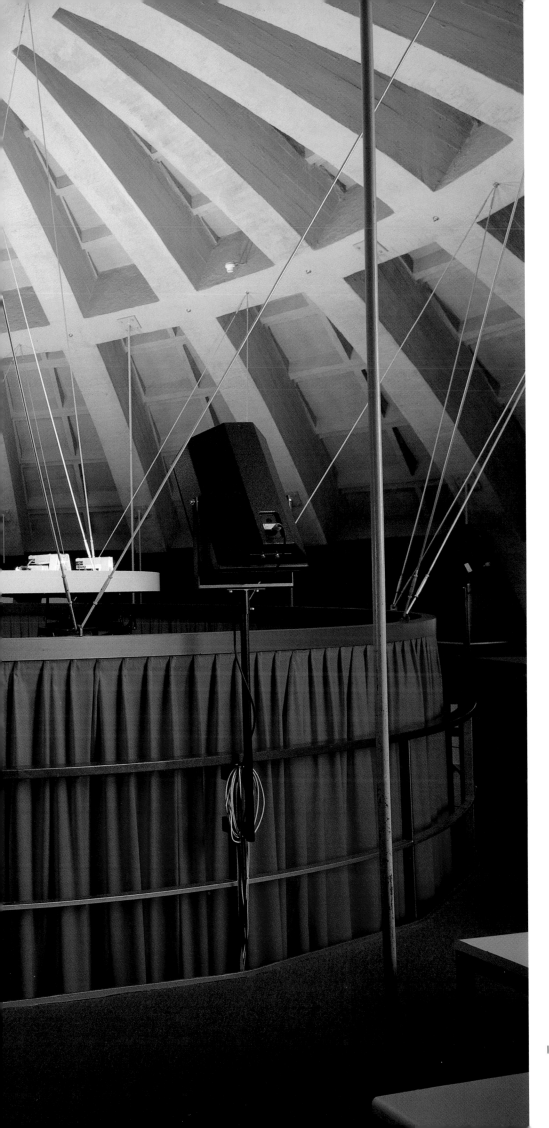

Interior of dome seen from the gallery

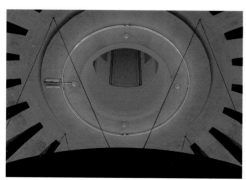

Detail views ▌ Reupholstered chairs by Ray and Charles Eames in front of the red curtain

of sight which meet in the lobby. The concealment of the building's innards allows its exterior to be received not as semiotic information, but as wittingly manipulated form, accessible to the viewing subject through the individuated act of formal perception. The revelation upon entry of all other information about the building reframes the viewing subject as part of a community. Form and program are distributed between separate perceptual experiences – outside and inside. The moment at which the two modes of perception coincide occurs on the threshold between interior and exterior.

The "postponement of semiotics"[2] in favor of the study of formal effect, which precedes the explication of the public realm at the school, is quite different from the simultaneous referentiality (external associations) and self-referentiality (inherent formal qualities) of the abstract forms employed in the dome. Nonetheless, the two projects share a syntax of materials, colors and details. While the ambition to foil semiotics may be seen in historical context as a response to the discourse of postmodernism, the regrounding of a vocabulary immanent to architecture – i.e., form – by recourse to both Gestalt psychological theory and historically grounded urban and building typology has much to do with the architects' biographies.[3] It has allowed them to develop a formal vocabulary

[2] Martin Steinmann, "Sensuality and Sense," *a + u* (5/96): 46.

[3] Their approach represents a marked departure from the movements which form the historical context of these two architects' training and early practice: post-1968 modernism and avant-gardism, and postmodernism. At the ETH Zurich, from which Christian Sumi graduated in 1977, the assumption which underlay the pedagogic approach was that "modernism has become teachable." See B. Hoesli, *Architektur Lehren*, gta (1983): 33. In place of an architecture which sought its first principles in "the play of pure forms in light," modernism was presented as a teachable,

which takes into account the perceptual effects of scale, context and abstraction. A palette of materials has emerged – comprising finely articulated surfaces and smooth, abstract planes, wood clad or plastered walls – which allows for manipulation of the apparent qualities of volumes and spaces by means of juxtaposition. It has also provided considerable insight into the relation between spatial forms and the historical context they reflect: the sequence through one project in particular, the addition to the Hotel Zürichberg, can be read as a concatenation of building and spatial typologies.[4]

To locate shifts in the model of reception on which the work relies, it is useful to consider the concept of the "ready-made." The term, coined to describe everyday culture's induction into the practice of (high) art, may be exemplified in architecture by Robert Venturi's Guild House (1960–63): the gilded TV antenna is as much a reminder of the retired tenants' favorite (low-cultural) activity as a reference to Jasper John's

repeatable architectural codex. As Sumi has pointed out in the interview quoted below, the realization that the tenets of modernism were to be seen as rules rather than eternal truths liberated architects from the ideology of truth in materials or functional expression. At the same time, however, it severed modernist form from its putative origins.

Modernism's institutional and formal codification was also the context for the work of the architectural avant-gardists of the late 1960s and 70s. The adaptation of such contemporary art practices as "happenings" was an attempt to critique this institutionalization. One example is Superstudio's "Hidden Architecture" (1970), in which blueprints of original drawings were sealed "forever" in a zinc box, the originals burned, and the notarized document bearing witness to that process exhibited. See *Design Quarterly (Conceptual Architecture)* 78/79 (1970): 54–57. Drawings, the bearers of the architect's originality and of his ability to communicate, were thus displaced by the gallery visitor's complicity: reception affirmed the fact of production, even in the absence of a physical product. The shift in focus from the production of architecture to the processes of its reception – from originality and singularity to communicability and the recession of the author-architect – and the potential of play in architecture are plausible points of reference for Burkhalter and Sumi: Marianne Burkhalter worked from 1969–78 several times with Superstudio in Florence and Studioworks in New York and Los Angeles.

[4] For a more detailed analysis, see "Hotel Zürichberg", *Daidalos (Sleeping Out)* (December 1996): 98–102.

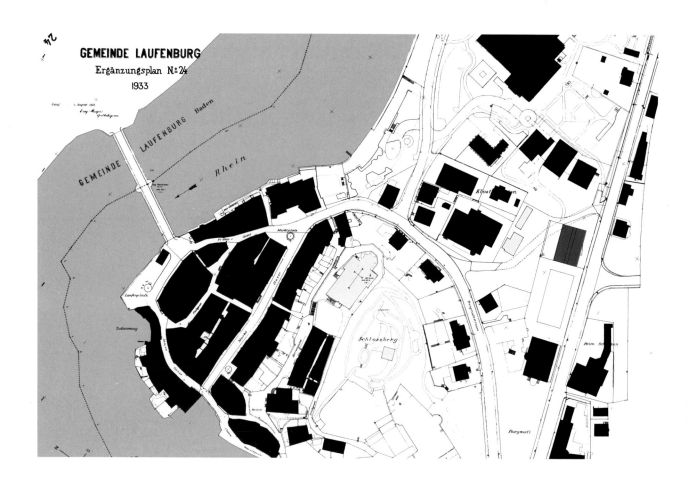

BUSINESS SCHOOL, LAUFENBURG, 1992

Competition 1989, 1st prize ▌ Client: The Municipality of Laufenburg ▌ Collaborators: Crispin Amrein, Adrien Froelich ▌ Project architects: Hürzeler und Winter, Magden ▌ Engineer: P. Schmid, Hägglingen

The new school is located opposite the old Burmatt schoolhouse and forms the termination of the school yard. The ground plan is structured in layers, as can be seen by the sectional view. The one-and-a-half-story-high entrance hall, "painted" with the complementary colors of red and green, forms the core of the complex. It receives light through the hallway, the faculty room and the large window facing Winterthurerstrasse; it is developed via the wedge-shaped lower entrance zone. The façade consists of horizontal wood lathing, or lamella, and serves as a backstop for the school yard. The west and south façades are conceived as uniform wooden shields and thus contradict the interior layered ground plan arrangement. The difficult relationship between the interior and the exterior, in the sense of the Venturis, between interior space, on the one hand, and the perception of the building volume from the outside, on the other, was an issue that concerned us greatly in this project, as it did with the kindergarten in Lustenau.

Street elevation and classroom façade

Façade facing the schoolyard ▶

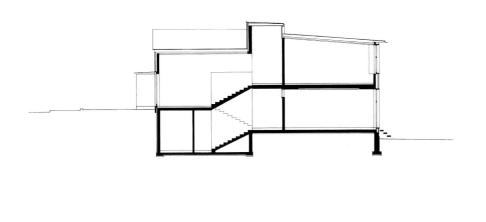

Cross section

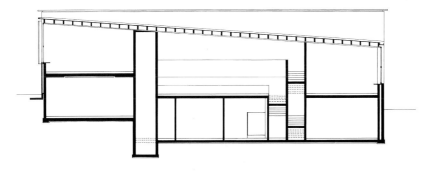

Longitudinal section

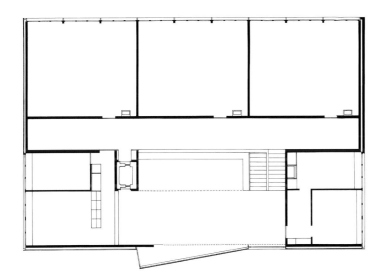

Entrance floor

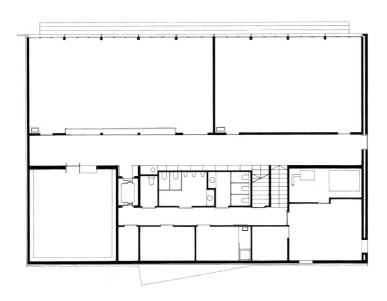

Courtyard level 1:300

Corridor and hall

Classroom ▌ Entrance and hall

bronzed Ballantine ale cans (1960).[5] In Burkhalter and Sumi's architectural vocabulary, the immediate recognizability of the quoted object as a commentary on the conventions of architecture is secondary. Instead, their ready-mades have taken the form of materials, extracted from their normative contexts, and therefore divorced from their normative referents, so as to question a semantic mode of reception. The cork-tiled entry wall in the Laufenburg Business School, for example, shares more with a cork floor in its finish and surface subdivisions than with a bulletin board. Another example cited by Sumi is the insertion of a larchwood window into an asphalt-tilted surface: "The tile has something of a sidewalk; at this point the associations begin to mingle. The wood and the asphalt reach a kind of equilibrum."[6]

The treatment of walls and portals as objects also serves to distance them from their normative referents. Door frames in the upper floor hallway are set flush with the wall to emphasize the counterpoised monolithic qualities and seemingly larger scale of that space – a manipulation of one's ability to judge relative size. In the addition to the Hotel Zürichberg, the ledge-like door saddles of the individual rooms operate in a similar manner. Juxtaposed with the smooth balustrade and wall surface of the interior spiral ramp, they create scalar conflict between the space, perceived as a larger-scale whole, and the presence of serial, finely articu-

[5] The influence of Venturi's theories of the "everyday" on Swiss architecture owes much to the periodical *archithese*, edited in the 70s by Stanislaus von Moos. Burkhalter and Sumi also cite the influence of the Smithsons, especially their *Without Rhetoric*.

[6] C. Sumi, *Daidalos (Magic of Materials II)* (August 1995): 30.

lated objects within that space. Furniture within the rooms comprises mobile objects, in which all scalar referents, such as doorpulls or hinges, have been repressed: the furniture, too, speaks to the perceptual issues of scalar disjuncture and volumetric composition. The mode of perception appropriate to these objectified elements can best be described with terms borrowed from Gestalt psychology.

With the repression of semantic meaning comes the loss of "everyday" associations – an acceptable, if not desirable, consequence for the kind of visual communication at issue in Gestalt perception theory. Gestalt theory presumes that the mode of perception which it describes is innate, and thus precedes the division of culture into high and low, into visual and verbal – if it does not precede culture entirely. Form, it argues, can be understood a priori as, for example, reclining or standing, dynamic or static, ordered or disordered;[7] reception is synonymous with a state in which "visual perception is the experience of visual forces."[8] But, in fact, formal literacy requires a shift from the usual, semantically grounded mode of reception to a mode which does not seek to understand meaning. Paradoxically, by attempting to move to a mode of perception which is universal, recourse to Gestalt psychology ends up requiring perhaps the least accessible of all modes of perception, that of individual aesthetic contemplation. In this sense, and in its demand that the distractions of

[7] A kind of illustrated primer of these categories was compiled by Martin Steinmann in collaboration with Walter Mair, *Daidalos (Positions in Space)* (March 1998): 26–35.

[8] Rudolf Arnheim, *The Dynamics of Architectural Form* (London: 1977), 44, quoted in Steinmann, op. cit., p. 47.

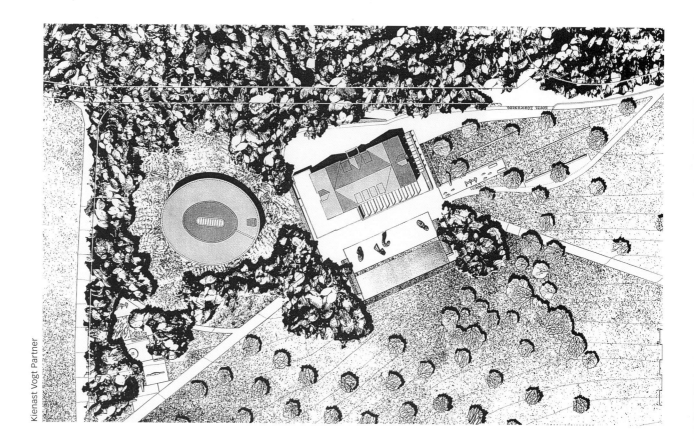

N

CONVERSION AND NEW BUILDING FOR HOTEL ZÜRICHBERG, ZURICH, 1995

Competition 1989, 1st prize ▌ Client: ZFV-Unternehmungen, Zurich ▌ Collaborators: Toni Wirth, Giorgio Bello, Marc Gilbert ▌ Project Architects: Arthur Schlatter, Rolf Schudel, Wernetshausen ▌ Engineer: J. Spahn, Zurich ▌ Landscape architects: Kienast Vogt Partner, Zurich

A continuous oval ramp generates the new building, which has a three-story, subterranean parking garage that "screws itself into the ground," and the two-story hotel tract that was placed over it, forming a lantern-like termination. The horizontal wooden façade clearly serves to distinguish the new building from the old brick structure. The new building becomes a type of pavilion in the former forest clearing, while the old structure remains at the center of the complex. In compliance with the clients' request to separate the hotel guests from guests who are merely on short excursions, the restaurant serving visitors on day trips was moved from the terrace to the garden floor. The central focus of the entrance floor is formed by the reception area, which was moved to the south in order to lead the arriving guests as quickly as possible to the terrace side, which offers a unique view of Zurich and the Alps. The various traditional hotel rooms – with such names as Resort Hall, Veranda Hall, and the former Restoration Hall – were all renovated in keeping with the original design. The park-like landscaping by Kienast Vogt Partners integrates the old complex by Mertens and creates a new whole.

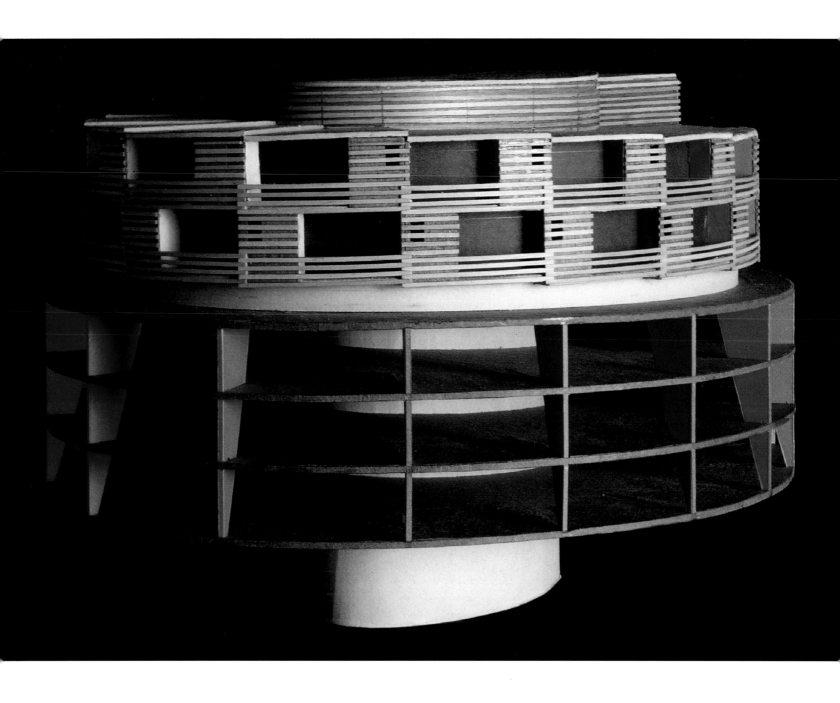

Model 1:100, and longitudinal section 1:800

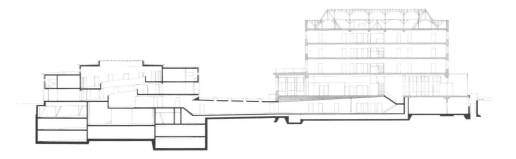

◄ Hotel lobby in the old building ▌ Sketch and exterior view with old building

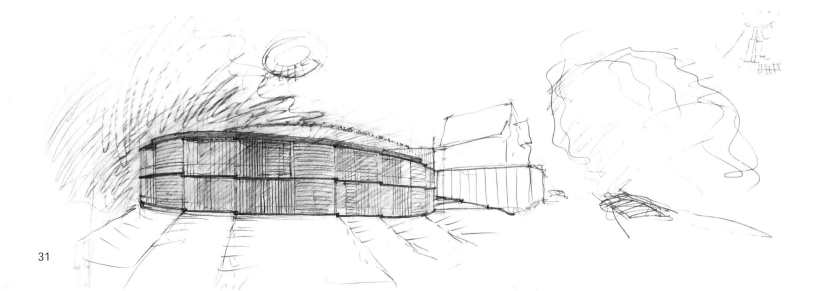

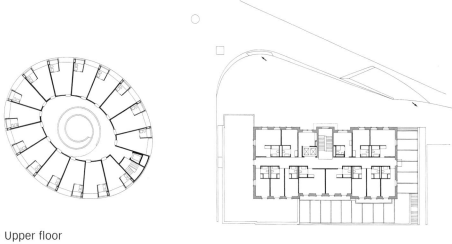

Upper floor

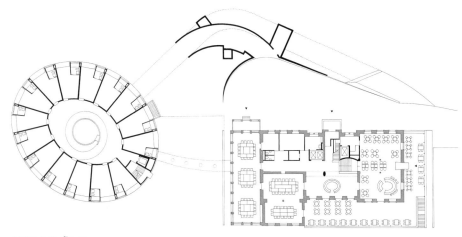

Entrance floor

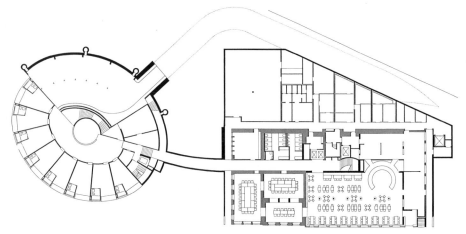

Garden level of old building

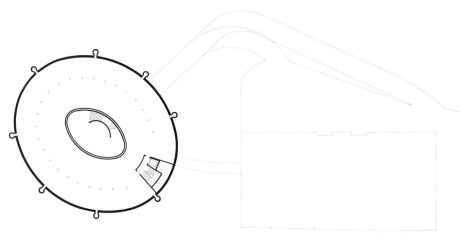

Parking for new building 1:800

Connecting corridor between

the old and new building ▶

Hall of new building

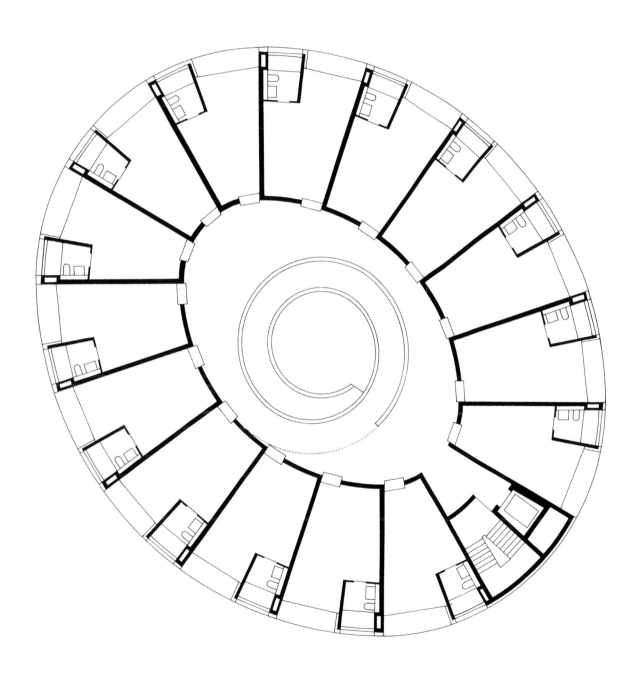

◀ Exterior view and room ▌ Ground plan 1:200

Screen

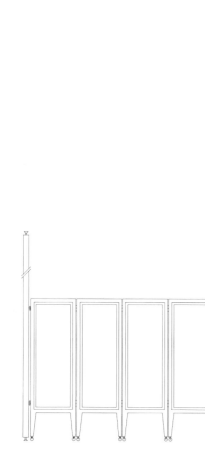

Mobile wardrobe

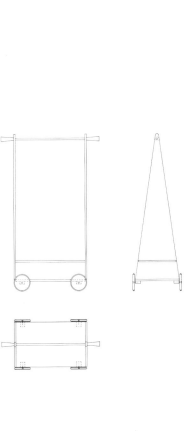

Bar stool

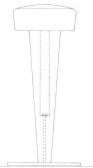

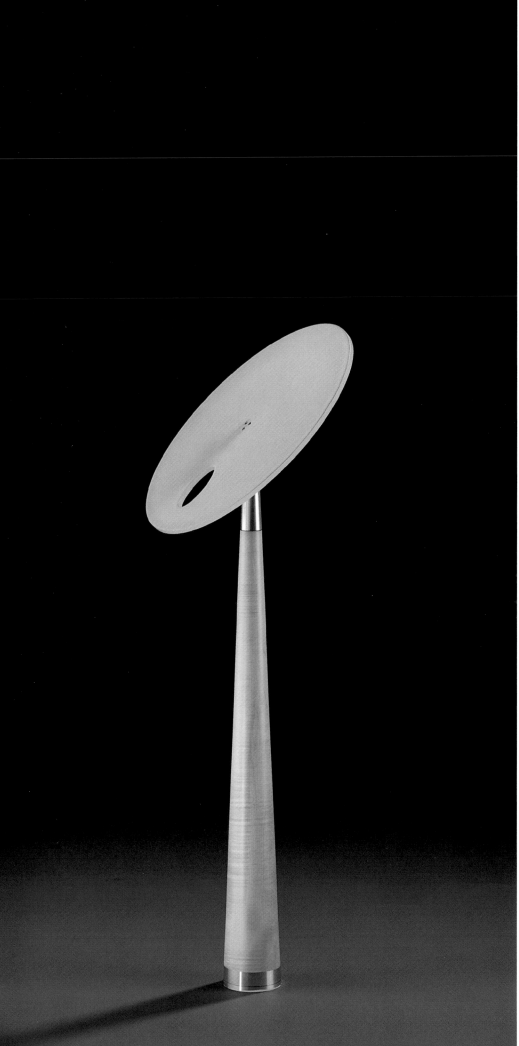

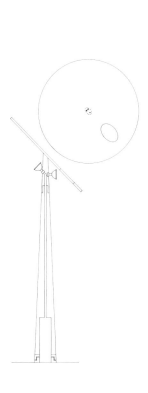

semantically based information be eliminated (or at least postponed), the architecture it dictates is high cultural in its trajectory. The same mandarinism may be inherent to the legibility of building typologies, which presume a common and homogeneous collective cultural memory. This qualification perhaps becomes only truly critical in the case of a public building, which depends so thoroughly on its communicative ability to effect a "space of public appearance." Consequently, with the broadening of the audience that results from the increasingly publicly accessible commissions with which Burkhalter and Sumi have recently dealt, the integration of other strategies tempers the Gestalt and the typological paradigms. The reworked proposal for a community center in Schwamendingen, an outlying area of Zurich, is emblematic.

The community center addresses the issue of the broad-based audience. Besides proper visitors, its audience also includes people who happen to live nearby or others who pass it in their cars. In this respect, it is less privileged than the Laufenburg school or the Hotel Zürichberg, which are directed primarily at a limited, receptive audience. Unlike these buildings, it has to draw its audience's attention. The community center expresses its status as a public amenity in subtle and less subtle ways. In contrast to its neighbors, which are positioned arbitrarily in relation to the primary streets, the building establishes an axial relationship to the main traffic artery. Its uncompromisingly prismatic massing and deep section are opposed to the episodic steppings and appendages of the housing around it. Whereas an earlier scheme attempted to ameliorate with the immediately adjacent youth club and with the scale of the context by embedding the large assembly hall into a slender z-shaped frame of wings, the latest scheme acknowledges its neighbor only in its orientation and axiality, but remains otherwise autonomous in a neoclassical vein of urbanism, which dealt with public buildings as urban monuments to be afforded distance.

The landscaping, designed in collaboration with Dieter Kienast and Günther Vogt, reinforces this relationship. A bracketing hedge extends from the edge of the existing building to the bicycle path, where it doubles back for a short stretch to end in a point. This hedge creates distance in several respects. It indicates that the gravel plaza belongs to the existing building rather than to the new, and that its spatial extent continues to the southwest.

The regularly articulated east façade of the community center forms the backdrop to the smaller ensemble of plaza, building and greenery. On the building's otherwise laconic exterior, provision has been made for large-scale signage – literal "ready-mades." The abstract exterior shell's tectonically modulated surface is robust enough to support this immediate, "low" cultural urban communication.

On the other side of the hedge is a paved platform raised half a flight above the plaza to afford a view back. Like many buildings by Marianne Burkhalter and Christian Sumi, the community center's façade is a carefully calibrated wood construction. Its framed structure is expressed tectonically by the regularly spaced, tall, thin windows. On the inside, the framing is articulated only by the floor joists, while the walls appear monolithic. The choice of material and the symmetrical disposition of rooms to one another and of building to site recall the ephemeral festival architecture of the 19th century. On the other hand, the exposed floor joists with their colored underside are both referential "ready-mades" and figures addressing abstract perceptual issues – a bridge between visual and cultural literacy. While they explicitly refer to the exposed woodwork of the medieval guild houses still familiar in the city of Zurich, they may also be read as a figure/ground striation of the floor plane or as a reiteration of the cross-axial movement which counters the primary orientation of the interior space.

The building's interior plays on the juxtaposition of symmetrical and serial elements. Beyond the entry, which barely disrupts the repetitive façade structure, the foyer is fronted by a continuous wall of doors, which again reiterate the bay structure. The assembly hall's axial symmetry is overlaid onto the serial bay rhythm. A balcony occupies the entrance wall. The far wall is wainscoted along its entire length by a wooden-slat bench – an element whose conflation of pew, garden furniture, and decorative woodwork is in itself a ready-made of sorts.

An entire series of typological associations is suggested by the hall, from the small concert hall in Schinkel's Schauspielhaus in Berlin to boxy Zwingli churches in Zurich, such as St. Peter's, to these churches' typological offspring, the Kongresshaus (by Haefeli, Moser, Steiger, 1939). The building is characterized by its capacity to address multiple audiences on its exterior and by its flexibility on the interior, which allows for countless variations on the relationship between audience and activity. These in turn allow for oscillation between an internal world of perception and an awareness of one's position as recipient – not at a single, privileged point, but in constant and shifting relationship to one's degree of participation in a public event.

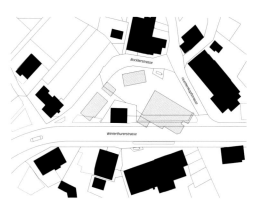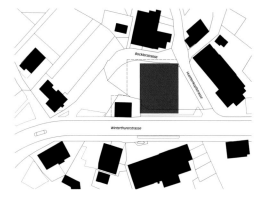

Situation in 1952 with Benzenhouse   Situation of Competition 1988   Situation of Project 1998

QUARTER CENTER, ZURICH-SCHWAMENDINGEN, PROJECT 1998

Competition 1998 ▌ Client: Building Department of the City of Zurich ▌ Collaborators: Nicole Baer ▌

Engineers: Branger, Conzett und Partner, Chur, Fietz AG, Zurich ▌ Landscape architects: Kienast Vogt Partner, Zurich

The straightening of Kantonstrasse in 1952 and the related demolishing of the Benzenhaus led to the definitive breakdown of the spatial unity of the old village center. The present design accepts and, at the same time, undermines the altered situation: the building volume, analogous to the restaurant Zur Eintracht (today a youth center), is oriented towards Kantonstrasse, but the entrance zone with foyer faces away from it and is positioned behind the youth center. The building intentionally takes up the tradition of the simple wooden theater and festival building, and presents a certain robustness and festive character that is appropriate for the building task – similar to the Théâtre du Jorat in Mézières, canton Vaadt, by Maillard + Chal (1907/08). The balconies can be used in many different ways, especially with the integration of the foyer floors behind them. Whereas the exterior spaces were explicitly differentiated and architecturally expressed in the competition project of 1988/1998, in the reworked version they are only "hinted at" by a single building volume. This "spatial" opening, in a certain sense, also reflects the "social" opening of the village over the past ten years: both the concerns of the traditional clubs, on the one hand, and the culturally creative, on the other, are today complemented and challenged by new multi-cultural demands of agglomeration. The social experiment of the site that is to be built involves the complex investigation of these various expectations, particularly in connection with the existing youth center.

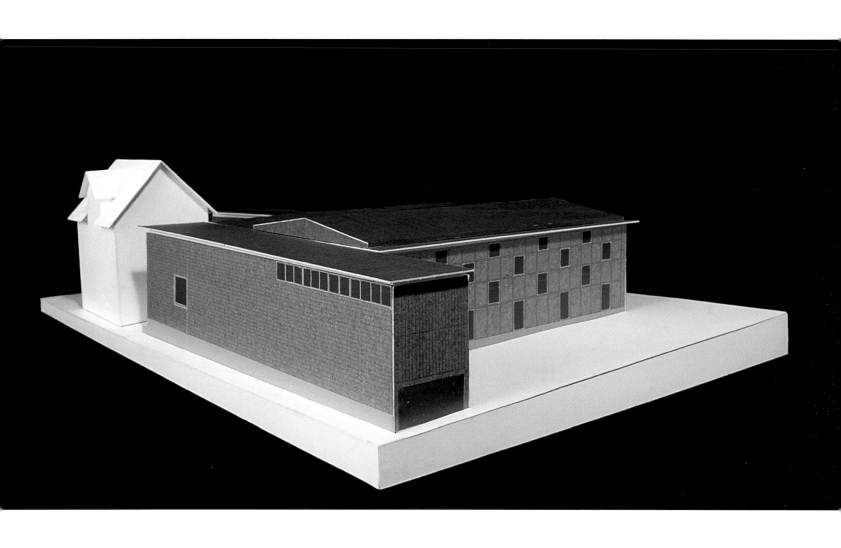

Model 1:100 competition 1988 ▌ Benzenhouse

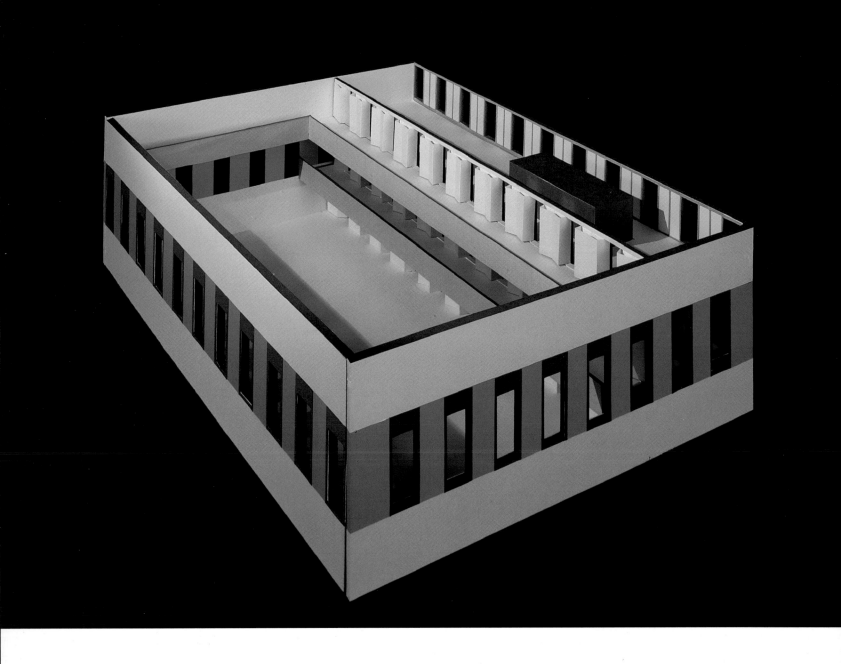

Model 1:50

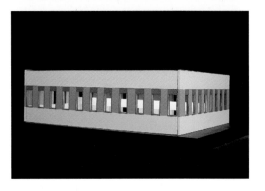

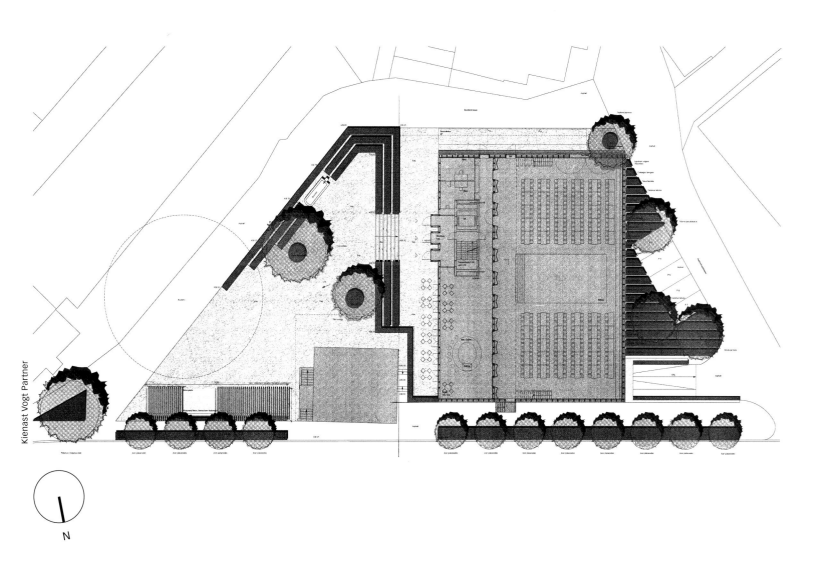

Klenast Vogt Partner

N

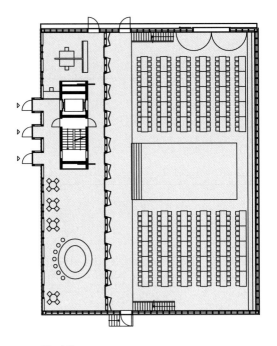

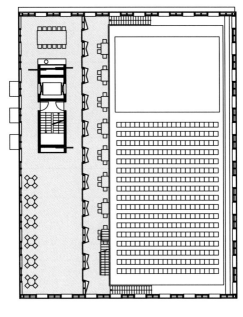

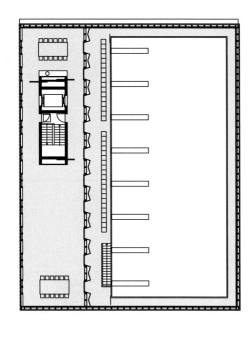

First floor

1st Upper floor

2nd Upper floor 1:400

Façade sketch ▋ Ground plan sketch ▶

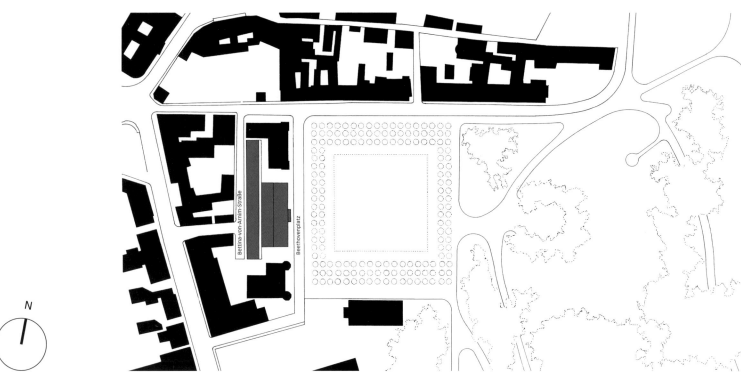

HOTEL DORINT, WEIMAR, 1998

Competition 1994, 1st prize ▮ Client: Dorint Hotel in Weimar GmbH + Co. KG ▮ General contractor: Hoch Tief ▮

Collaborators: Bard Helland, Michael Fischer

The conversion of the two lateral buildings into their original angular formation allows the new building volume to be differentially integrated into the existing substance. Given the asymmetrical interlocking of the rows of rooms, the project becomes a mediating link between Beethovenplatz and Bettina-von-Arnim-Strasse. The strikingly expressive attic floor structures the façade and integrates it into the roof silhouette of the two corner volumes. A classical light-dark striation "covers up" the energy-efficient exterior insulation, and the planted yard façade forms the "natural" background for this striation, endowing the building with an appropriate representation. The square, too, has been redesigned in connection with the construction of a circular parking garage beneath Beethovenplatz that provides access to the hotel. The present project was realized by a general contractor in accordance with the building order.

Building volume with attic floor ▌ Frontal view from Beethovenplatz

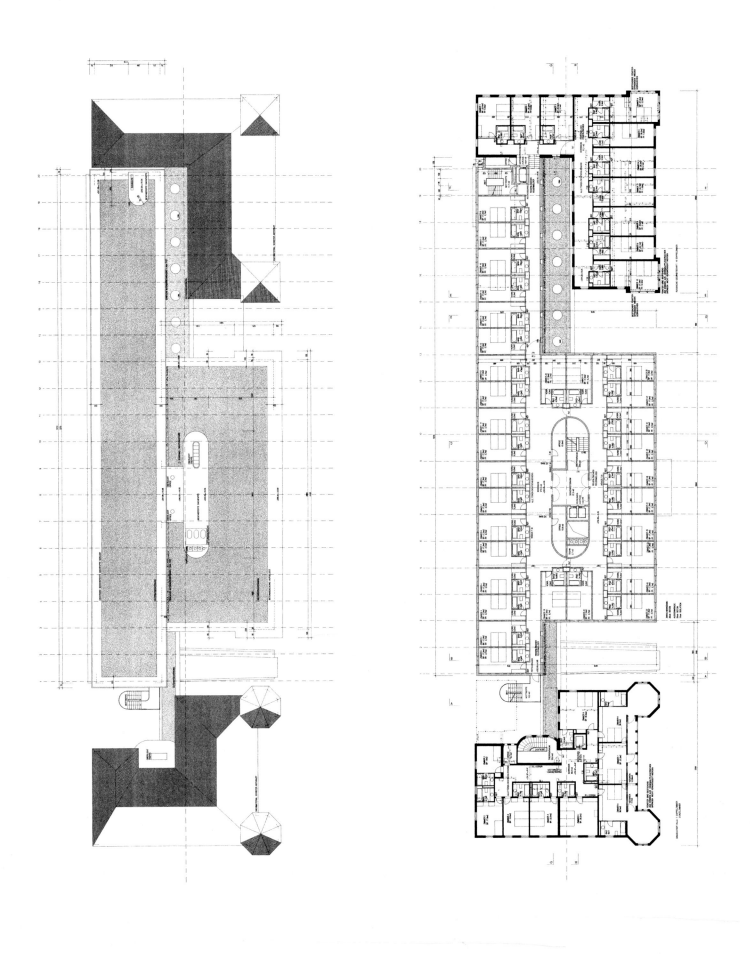

Roof elevation and upper floor ▌ View into Bettina-von-Armin-Strasse ▶

APARTMENT BUILDINGS – FORMS OF LIVING

STEVEN SPIER

The provision of shelter is a fundamental act, and is thus an especially demanding and revealing brief for the architect and the society in which he or she works. This has been particularly so since industrialization transformed the provision of shelter into the problem of housing, when architecture was forced to confront the question of how it should respond to the changing nature of how we live. For, as the work that follows confirms, the architectural implications of the considerable contemporary social changes in the industrialized world – including the continuing dissolution of the traditional family, the declining distinction between home and work, locations which are not simply urban, suburban, or rural – are not self-evident. Certainly the diversity of sites, programs, clients, and occupants to which the projects in this chapter responds precludes any concise response. The architect is left with the dilemma of how to ground his or her work in something more nourishing than the architect's own ego, the demands of the client, or the expediency of style. Housing, being an unpropitious vehicle for purely formal or personal expression, makes this dilemma especially compelling.

That the problem of housing is a problem for the architect is tautological in some countries but is remarkable seen from the United States or Great Britain, where the form of how we shall live is the province of developers and builders; and the object of their production is emphatically the single-family house. That this type no longer provides a practical solution to

57

current housing needs[1] only confirms its cultural significance.[2] It is remarkable in London, for example, how narrow the breadth of housing choice is. Rather than apartments built expressly for the middle class, there are nineteenth-century terrace houses converted to flats. The visible building material for a home, existing or new, must be brick. Modern housing with modern space exists almost solely in social housing,[3] though even this modest development of the problem was ended in 1979, when the Conservative Party won the general election. A generation of architects has come of age with no experience in designing housing.[4]

For Burkhalter and Sumi housing is, of course, part of their practice as architects, and the project in Laufenburg shows how their work accepts its complexities. Here the program is socially mixed, and the site is neither urban-dense and small-grained, nor suburban-atomized and uniform,

[handwritten: contradicts previous pages' reference to distinct "declining home between work and locations."]

[1] Its inherently low density is hardly compatible with the (length of commute) and the price of land it engenders, nor the atrophy of the profession of full-time parent. The village model put forward by the traditionalists cannot hope to accommodate changing demographics, nor what can only be described in Britain as a crisis: there is an estimated need for 4.4 million new homes over the next 20 years, of which 80% will be occupied by single people. The obvious response of increasing urban densities has been contentious in the popular and professional press, with grave doubts as to the appeal of what is regarded uncomfortably as urban living.

[2] For a readable history, see Robert Fishman, *Bourgeois Utopias: The Rise and Fall of Suburbia* (New York: 1987). For the cultural significance of the arcadian dream and suburbia in the United States, see Leo Marx, *The Machine in the Garden: Technology and the Pastoral Ideal in America* (New York: 1964).

[3] Though such flats may be bought and sold, their much lower value and the near impossibility of attaining a mortgage on a flat higher than the fifth floor accurately reflects social values and a contempt for modernism itself. Tellingly, social housing in Britain is called council housing after the local government level, which is widely ridiculed; in the U.S., it is called public housing in a society where the notion of the public is debased. A 1952 referendum in Los Angeles, for instance, virtually prohibited public housing. It was seen as socialistic.

[4] Housing has lately raised its profile in Britain, as can be seen in the Millennium Village competition for Greenwich Peninsula. It is also tentatively reentering schools of architecture. But it is still largely the province of specialized firms, and its development by the profession at large has been broken.

dependent on the automobile. Both circumstances are then ambiguous in their balance between public and private, an ambiguity Burkhalter and Sumi give form to by drawing on the example of gallery access housing.[5] The architects accept and articulate an ambivalence in the relative value of public and private space, in the collective versus the individual, with a gallery that functions as both circulation and communal space. They *COMMON* modify the modernist version with its emphatic privileging of the functionality by combining it with a rural model where the gallery is understood as social.[6] *COMMON* The internal organization likewise accepts this complexity, rejecting the modernists' clear partitioning into day and night zones. This then requires some ingenuity to ensure privacy, which is achieved here by cutting shafts through the floor of the gallery, entry pieces which form less public spaces, and the careful placing of windows. At ground level the building likewise defines a weak public space. On the south side, it is green; on the north side, the architects have the wit to use the automobile to create another gallery by veiling the open garage facing the shopping center with a green scrim of chain-link fence. The building technology is freed from ideological and cultural imperatives and so can be used to optimize responses to structural, environmental, social, and

[5] Even this ambivalence might seem emphatic within a culture which could applaud Thatcher for saying, "There is no such thing as society." Martin Steinmann traces gallery access housing's evolution from Streatham Street in London in 1849/50 through the Smithsons' Golden Lane Housing and Rossi's Gallaratese in "Das Laubenganghaus: Bemerkungen zu seinem Bedeutungswandel zwischen 1849 und 1929," in *archithese (Das Kollektivwohnhaus)* 12 (1974).

[6] The modernist solution huddled the kitchen, bathroom, and bedrooms off a narrow entrance gallery on the north side with the apartment opening up to a large room with generous glazing and a balcony towards the south. The social space was nominally the stairway. In the alpine typology the gallery is broad and faces south. People congregate on this sunny side to socialize, work, and dry crops.

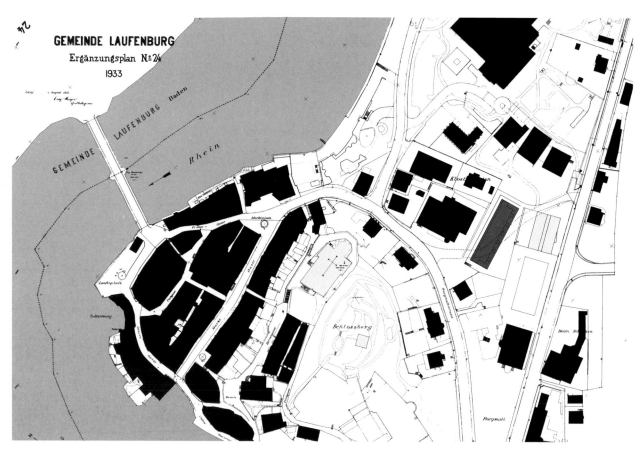

Remarks ▮ Site size: approx. 20 000 square feet ▮ Floors: 3 ▮ Use: 1.0

SOUTH GALLERY HOUSE, LAUFENBURG, 1996

Competition 1989, 1st prize ▮ Client: Housing Cooperative Laufenburg ▮ Collaborators: Robert Albertin ▮

Project Architects: Rene Birri, Stein am Rhein ▮ Engineer: Koch und Schmid, Laufenburg ▮ Landscape architects: Kienast Vogt Partner, Zurich

The 16 cooperative apartments in Laufenburg are part of the housing project sponsored by the state in accordance with the housing and owner-ship sponsoring law (WEG). The oversized arcade is situated on the south side and combines the access with the exterior space belonging to the apartment – an unusual overlapping of private and public use in Switzerland. But the fact that all the apartments had already been rented prior to the completion of the building refutes certain narrow-minded ideas of social housing and rewards the openness of the client. In collaboration with Erne in Laufenburg, we developed a wood façade element which costs no more than the traditional Eternit-paneled walls. The precondition was that the junctions be rigorously standardized and the order for both the façade elements and the wooden windows be placed with the same company.

South gallery with the entrance zones

Upper floor

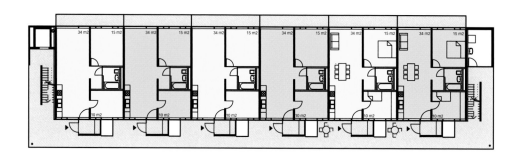

Entrance floor

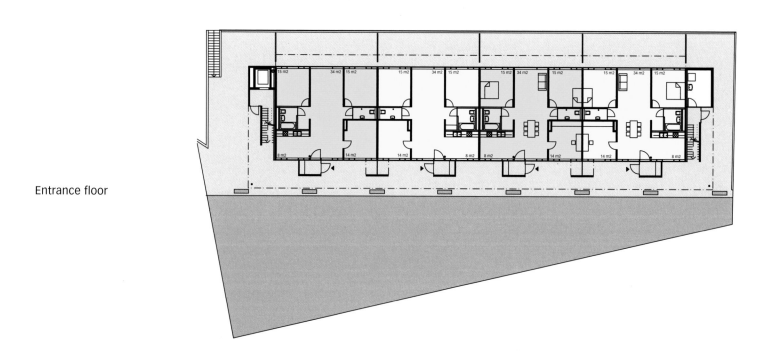

Parking 1:400

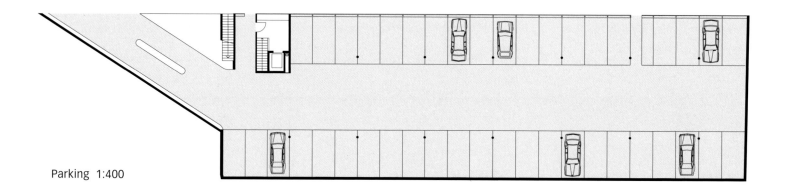

South gallery

North side with ground-level parking

Cross section of stairway

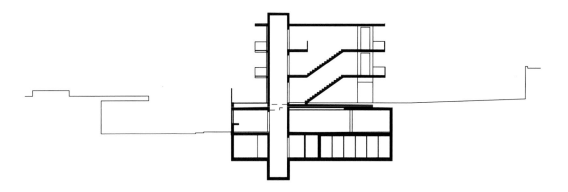

Cross section of apartments

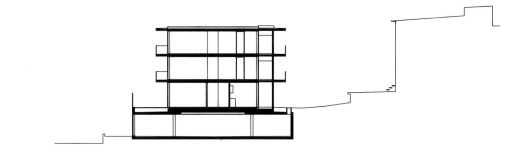

South façade

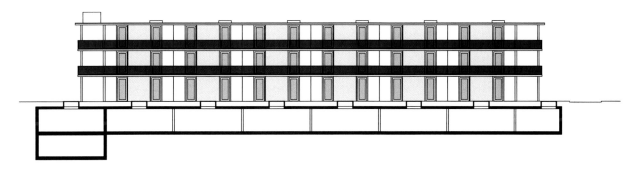

North façade 1:400

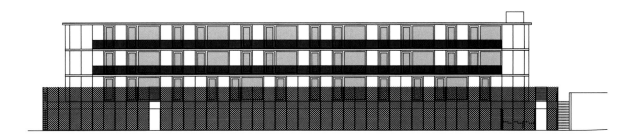

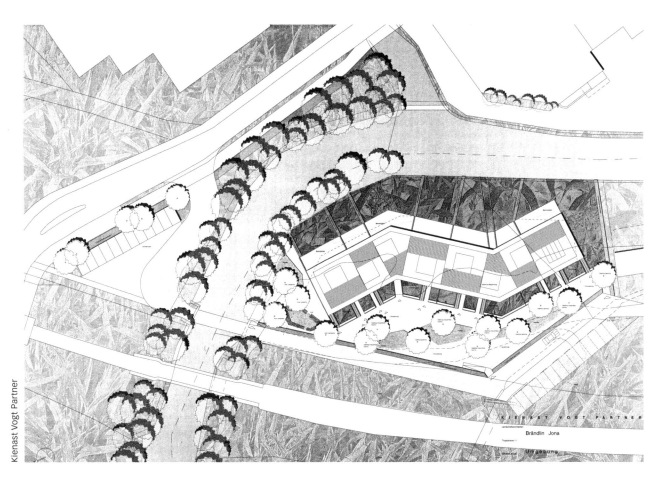

Kienast Vogt Partner

Remarks ▮ Site size: approx. 42 000 square feet ▮ Floors: 2 + attic ▮ Use: 0.45

GALLERY HOUSE, RAPPERSWIL, PROJECT 1998

Client: Braendlin AG, Jona ▮ Collaborators: Claudia Murer, Maja Mileticki, Hamos Meneghelli ▮ Landscape architects: Kienast Vogt Partner, Zurich

The railroad tracks demarcate the area occupied by the former Nachtweid: spatial references and chambers have been neutralized and fragmented. The present project attempts to provide the remaining area in the north with an identity and to integrate it into the converted textile industrial area. The building volume has been broken, or "jolted," twice and occupies the center of the site with the outdoor stairs that provide access to the upper floor. Various views open up as a result of the bends in the building volume. Some parking is provided at the entrance; the rest is located in the wind shadow of the railroad embankment.

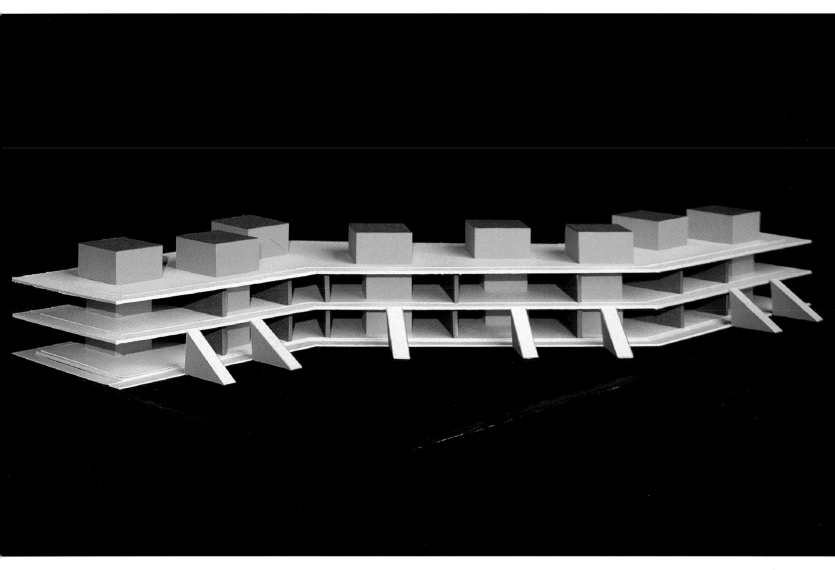

Façades 1:400 and model 1:100

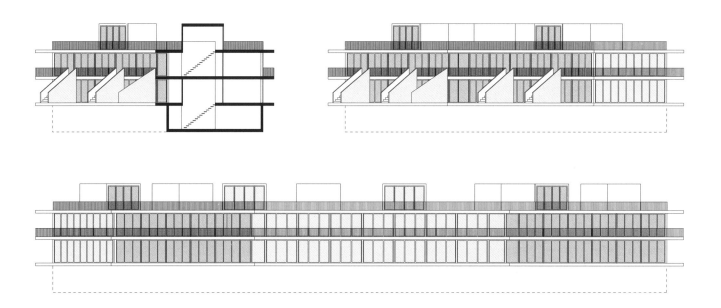

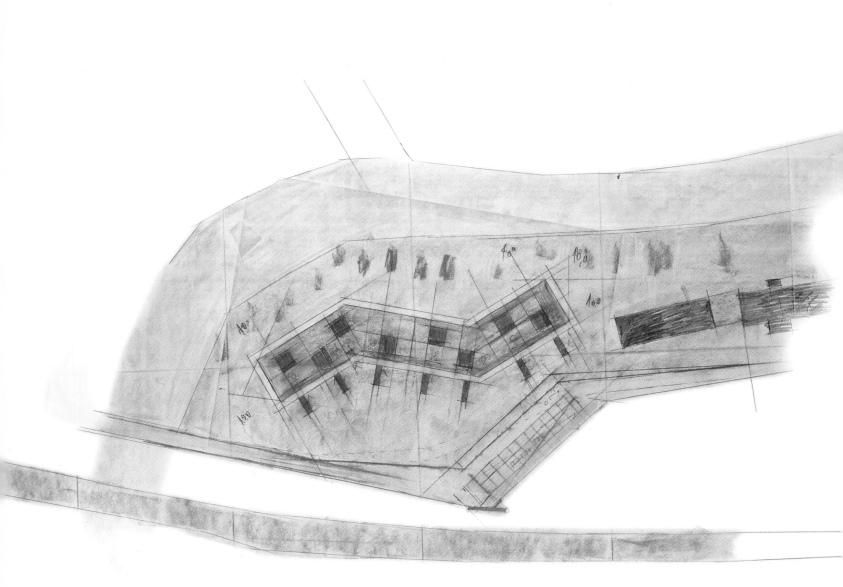

Attic

Upper floor

First floor 1:400

formal concerns. A similar pragmatism embraces the expediency and economy of applied color to reinforce social and formal issues.

In Laufenburg, then, we see a way of approaching the architectural problem of housing that accepts its multifarious, often contradictory components. We can also discern a method of working, though not a methodology, that is grounded in something larger than the individual object or subject. This method of modification "reveals an awareness of being part of a pre-existing whole, of changing one part of a system to transform the whole ... Thus the specificity of the solution is closely related to differences in situation, context or environment."[7] It is a position which refutes the notion of the building as the simple repository of genius, while nevertheless demanding considerable intellect and invention. It necessitates a continuous engagement with and thus evolution of the problem, however, and some certainty as to the tradition upon which one is building (which in Switzerland is a strand of modernism). Burkhalter and Sumi's engagement with the terrace house shows how fertile these conditions can be.

At Köpenick the architects confronted a need for low-density housing in the flat landscape of woods and lakes near Berlin. Clearly, the brief suggests a strategy of objects in the landscape, but here the object chosen is terrace housing. While, on the one hand, a sensible choice of typology – it does balance the part and the whole, the desire for an individual house and for community – the choice of an urban typology in such a setting is nevertheless provocative. It proves itself, though, well able to adapt to

[7] Vittorio Gregotti, "Territory and Architecture", *Architectural Design Profile* (London) 59, no. 5–6 (1985): 28.

contemporary needs and needs unforeseen. Within this choice, the architects devise two types, each of which has two variations, which they join into a larger mass. The terrace house, with its unambiguous zoning of front and rear, is stretched to form instead three pieces: the living core, a court, and a smaller, detachable unit. These parts can be one-story or two-story and arranged in various orientations to provide for a variety of uses: home office, study, guest room, hobby room, separate apartment. The various configurations and parts are then unified in the façade.

The site in Erfurt lies outside the existing city, but the infrastructure in place acknowledges its eventual incorporation as a new quarter of town. The physical context is rich – a southerly aspect on the highest point in the area – while the budget was stringent, demanding considerable spatial efficiency. Burkhalter and Sumi again work with the type of terrace housing as in Köpenick but siting it more conventionally. The bulk of the scheme is a two-story terrace house organized conventionally as a dumbbell. The architects have added a detached one-story structure, the position and dimension of which creates a flexibility of use.

Typology is a contentious term in the U.S. and Britain, with a remarkable lack of consensus even as to its meaning. It is generally understood as a taxonomy – of function, of tectonics (often structural), or of form. It is often taken to mean a catalogue of solutions to architectural arrangement and is debased as a pattern book of architectural language or materials.[8]

---

[8] Aldo Rossi's use of typology as a definitive criticism of functionalism, for instance, seems either hopelessly nostalgic or plain daft in a culture which, devoted to brave new worlds, so exalts the individual.

86 ▶

Remarks ▮ Site size: 122 000 square feet ▮ Floors : 2 ▮ Use: 0.4

CONDENSED HOUSING, BERLIN-KÖPENICK (GERMANY), COMPETITION 1997,

IN COOPERATION WITH REGINA BÖHM, DANIELA DÄUMLER, TOBIAS HAAG, WEIMAR

Contractor: Merk Systembau GmbH, Füssen, Germany ▮ Landscape architects: Kienast Vogt Partner, Zurich

A beautiful forest with sandy soil and the lakes nearby create a comfortable atmosphere which, especially considering the relatively low level of use, needs to be respected and even enhanced: four housing groups of different sizes form casual neighborhood units that "float" like islands in the birch and pine forest. The houses consist of core buildings similar to those in Erfurt, but the side houses are conceived in quite a different manner: in the case of the 5.0 m type, they are connected on one floor with the core house; in the case of the 3.75 m type, they are separated on two floors from the core house. Depending on the location of the parking lot or house entrance, the side houses become front or rear houses.

Elevations ▮ Model 1:200

Type 5.00 m

Façade

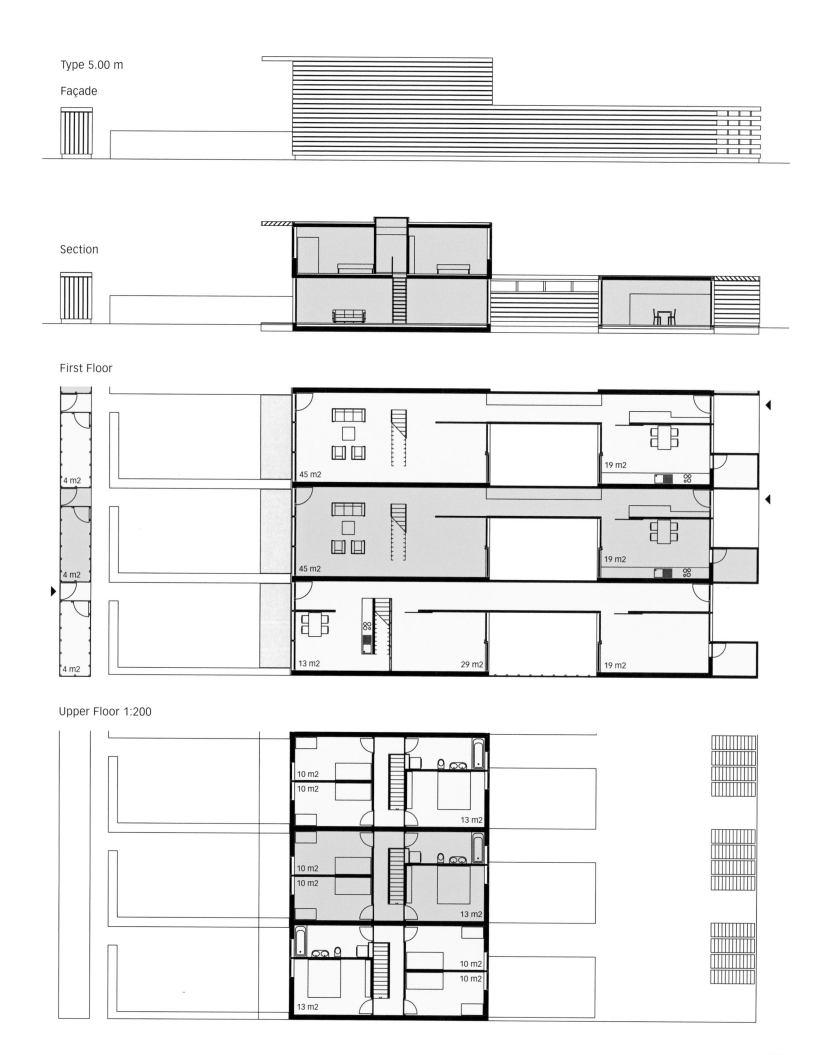

Section

First Floor

4 m2

4 m2

4 m2

45 m2

45 m2

19 m2

19 m2

13 m2

29 m2

19 m2

Upper Floor 1:200

10 m2

10 m2

13 m2

10 m2

10 m2

13 m2

13 m2

10 m2

10 m2

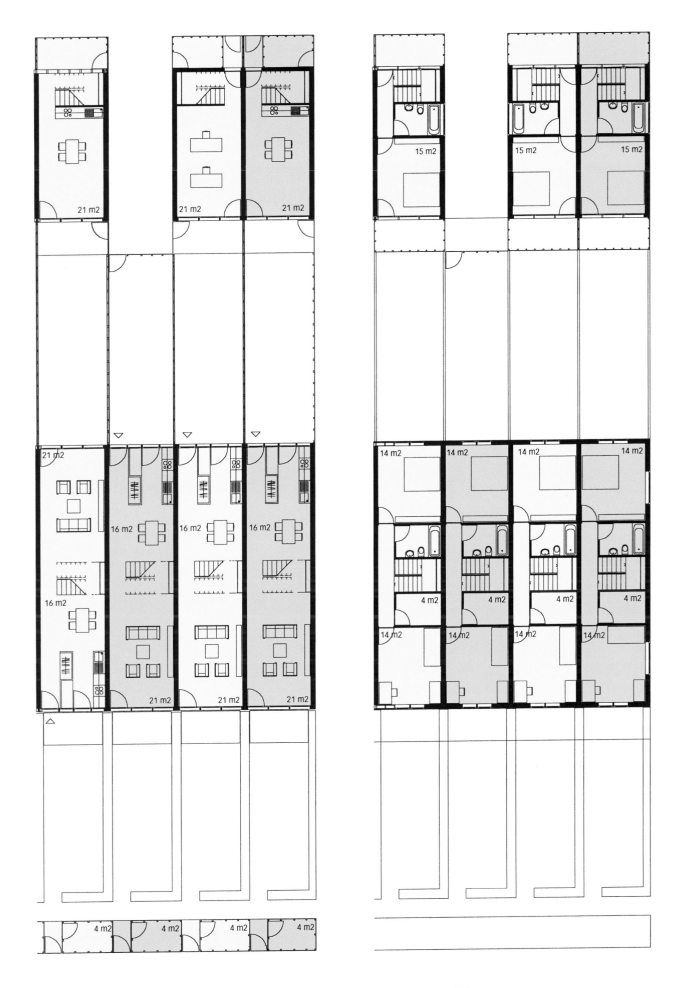

Type 3.75 m   First Floor

Upper Floor 1:200

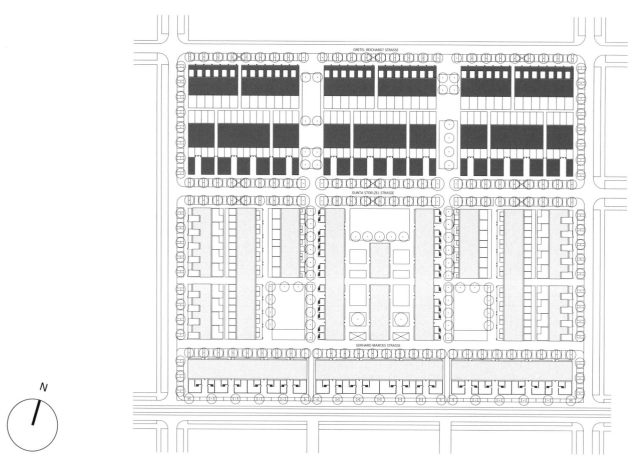

Remarks ▎ Site size: approx. 49 000 square feet ▎ Floors : 2 ▎ Use: 0.9

CONDENSED HOUSING, ERFURT-RINGELBERG, GERMANY, PROJECT 1998,

IN COOPERATION WITH REGINA BÖHM, DANIELA DÄUMLER, TOBIAS HAAG, WEIMAR

1st phase, Competition 1995: Regina Böhm, Daniela Däumler, Tobias Haag, Stefan Kastner ▎ 2nd phase, Competition 1995:

as above, in cooperation with Burkhalter + Sumi ▎ Building Project 1996: as above (without Stefan Kastner) ▎ Client: Landesentwicklungs-

gesellschaft LEG Thüringen Ltd. ▎ Engineer: Bauart Stefan Winter, Lauterbach, Germany

The planned complex forms the northern termination of a development that we conceived in conjunction with Atelier 5 in Bern. The single-story

projections of the two rows of houses oriented along a north-south axis define the street space. A continuous "green zone" is to evolve between

the rows. Two different, standardized building types were suggested as "core" houses:

Type 5.10 m – The broad and short "classical" row house with a single-flight, transversely placed staircase that was extended into an atrium

space due to the storage room and located towards the street, and a glazed foyer.

Type 4.0 m – The narrow and long "modernist" row house with a double-flight transversely placed staircase that was extended into a yard house

due to an autonomous garden room.

The houses are conceived as modern wooden structures; those by Atelier 5 consist of prefabricated concrete elements. This project will not be

realized.

Model 1:100

Type 4.00 m

Façade

Section

First Floor

22 m2

18 m2

7 m2 | 4 m2

22 m2

7 m2 | 4 m2

18 m2

22 m2

22 m2

7 m2 | 4 m2

20 m2

22 m2

22 m2

18 m2

22 m2

Upper Floor 1:200

15 m2 | 15 m2

15 m2 | 15 m2

15 m2 | 15 m2

15 m2 | 15 m2

Type 5.10 m

Façade

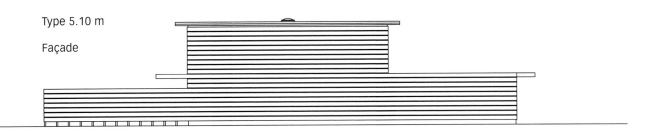

Section

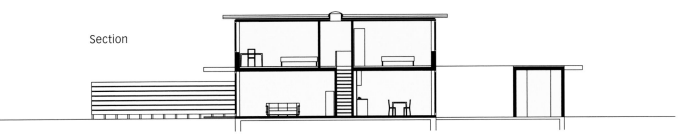

First Floor

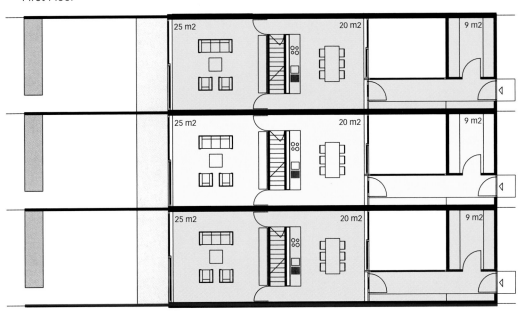

Upper Floor 1:200

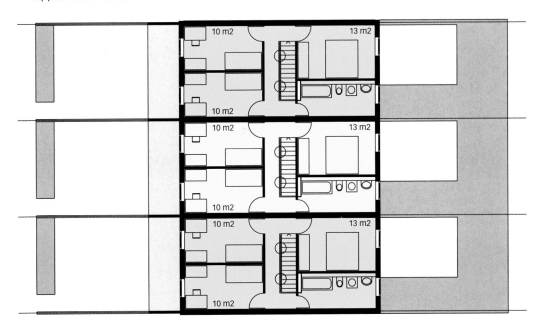

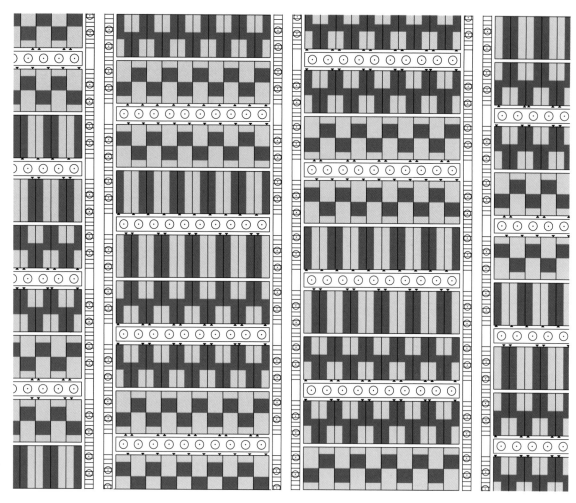

N

Remarks ▌ Site size: approx. 20 660 square feet (10 units) ▌ Floors: 1 ▌ Use: 0.5 (full extension)

CONDENSED HOUSING IN BRAZIL, STUDY 1999

Client: EuroPartner do Brasil, Rio de Janeiro ▌ Collaborators: Jürg Schmid, Claudia Murer, Barbara Ruppeiner, Andrea Calanchini

The parcel has a size of 8 X 24 m and is situated either along or crosswise to the street. It generates different, one-story minimal core houses such as, for example, the yard house, the double-yard house, the atrium house and the square house. The houses can be extended up to half the size of the property, either as living spaces or as workspaces for businesses and workshops.

The houses are joined together along green zones into neighborhood clusters of 10 or 20 units. The infrastructure – for example, healthcare, schools, bus terminals and soccer fields – is located in vacant building lots or clusters. Following the "house" and the "neighborhood" it forms the third urban level. The houses are realized as modern low-tech wooden constructions.

Models double-yard house 1:50

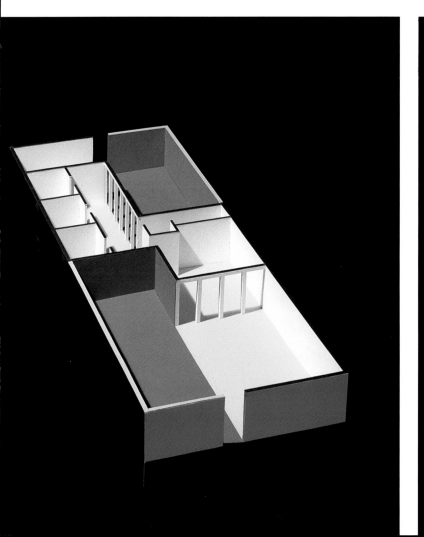

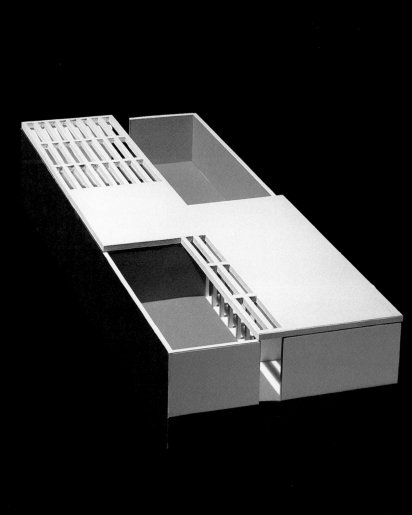

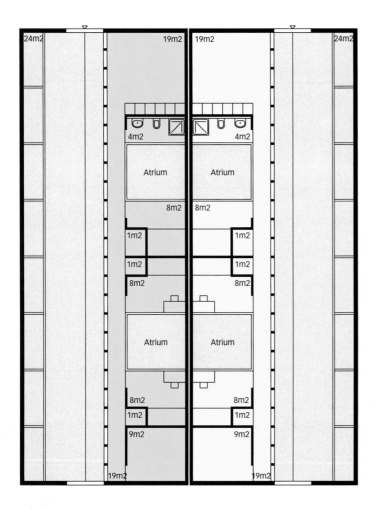

Ground plan atrium house

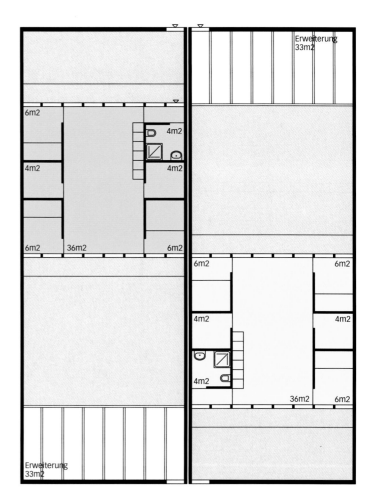

Ground plan single-room house

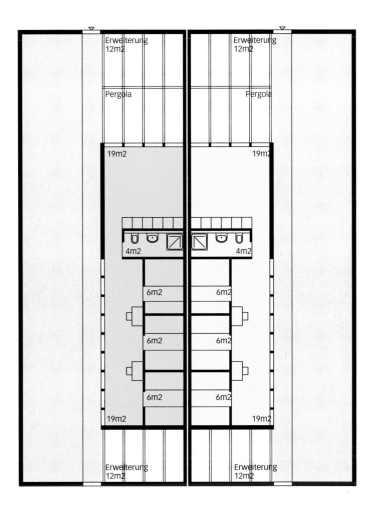

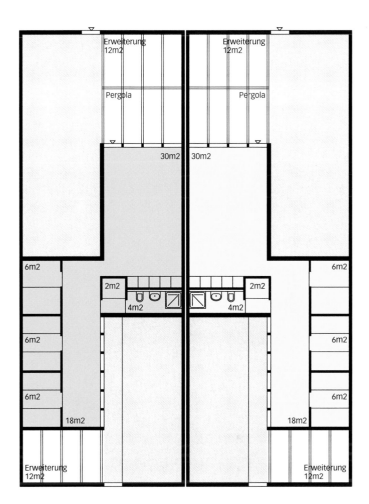

Ground plan yard house

Ground plan double-yard house 1:200

But a more profound understanding of typology, as a category of forms available for transformation, can provide architecture with depth and rigor, where "there is no clear set of rules for the transformations and their objects, nor any polemically defined set of historical precedents. Nor should there be; the continued vitality of this architectural practice rests in its essential engagement with the precise demands of the present ... It refuses any "nostalgia" in its evocations of history ... it refuses all unitary descriptions of the social meaning of form ... it finally refuses all eclecticism, resolutely filtering its "quotations" through the lens of a modernist aesthetic."[9] As we shall see clearly in the next two schemes, this understanding of typology provides a discipline within which one can work inventively. It allows Marianne Burkhalter and Christian Sumi to reject universal solutions in favor of specific ones which are nevertheless not completely singular.[10]

The projects in Herrliberg and in Melchrüti are, at first glance, suburban developments on greenfield sites within easy commuting distance of the historical city. But the different programs, in each case set by the developer in response to site and market considerations, suggested neither single-family villas nor multi-family housing but a hybrid. Herrliberg is in an exclusive, wooded area outside of Zurich with a southern aspect and views

[9] A. Vidler, "The Third Typology." Reprinted in Kate Nesbitt, ed., *Theorizing a New Agenda for Architecture: An Anthology of Architectural Theory 1965–1995* (New York: 1996): 263.

[10] An example of such work would be Le Corbusier's surprisingly accommodating and ultimately fruitful attitude towards the client's criticisms of his initial scheme for the Maison Clarté. The radical changes from the initial proposal not only satisfy the client, but further the architect's broader research. See Sumi, *Immeuble Clarté Genf 1932 von Le Corbusier & Pierre Jeanneret* (Zurich: 1989).

of the lake; it demands luxury – here in the form of space, exclusivity, privacy, and view. Placing the mass of the building so that it is either perpendicular or parallel to the slope relates one to the topography and helps maintain views while gently contradicting the unity of form in mass, materials, and color. These two orientations are then developed as formal types. Divided either lengthwise or crosswise, they provide a variety of external spaces, internal configurations, and relationships that help assert their individuality. The structural system is designed to reinforce this spatial and programmatic flexibility.

At Melchrüti the architects were responding to a different socioeconomic context, a marginal area of postwar sprawl near the airport, where the developer needed apartments that would appeal to an urbane, middle-class public, and decreed large, affordable apartments with great flexibility of use.

Marianne Burkhalter and Christian Sumi recognize the problem of dispersal and loss of identity in such a context, accepting it almost typologically without commending it. The architects work again within a discipline of two types, here formal reversals of each other. In one, the circulation occupies the central space, a postwar typology of a central core. This creates a cellular plan that is bifurcated in either one or both directions. Consistent with this approach, the elevations are relatively uniform and relate to the internal organization. The other type leaves the central space unoccupied with the circulation reduced to one of four service cores dispersed to the perimeters. As in a Palladian villa, this strategy creates the figure of a cross, though here the space is flowing and modernist,

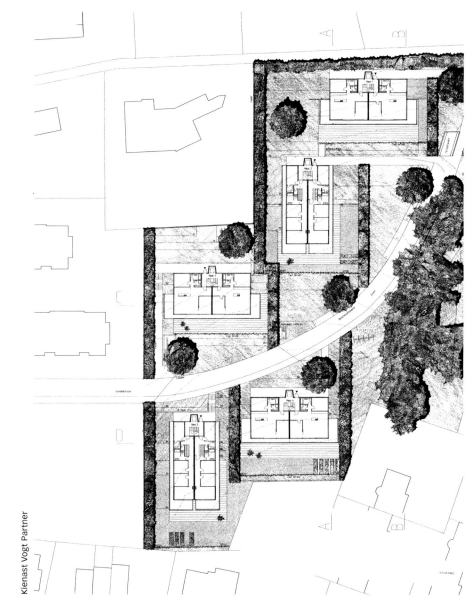

N

Kienast Vogt Partner

Remarks ▍ Site size: approx. 82 000 square feet ▍ Floors: 2 + attic ▍ Use: 0.5

TOWN VILLAS, HERRLIBERG, PROJECT 1997

Competition 1995, 1st prize ▍ Client: Göhner Merkur Immobilien AG, Zurich ▍ Collaborators: Hermann Kohler ▍
Landscape architects: Kienast Vogt Partner, Zurich

The open, single-family housing complex accentuates and respects the slightly sloping, ravine-like external landscape – the grounds avoid becoming cut off from the outside environment – and conforms to the dimensions of the houses in the existing development.

Each house is separated along the fall line. Their varying orientations – crosswise or parallel to the slope – offer differentiated apartment types: either square or linear. Both apartments and duplexes are feasible. Building entrances, via stairs or elevators, are located outside each building on the side of the slope. Strongly cantilevered, uninterrupted balconies in the style of Frank Lloyd Wright's Usonian houses mediate between the interior and the exterior spaces.

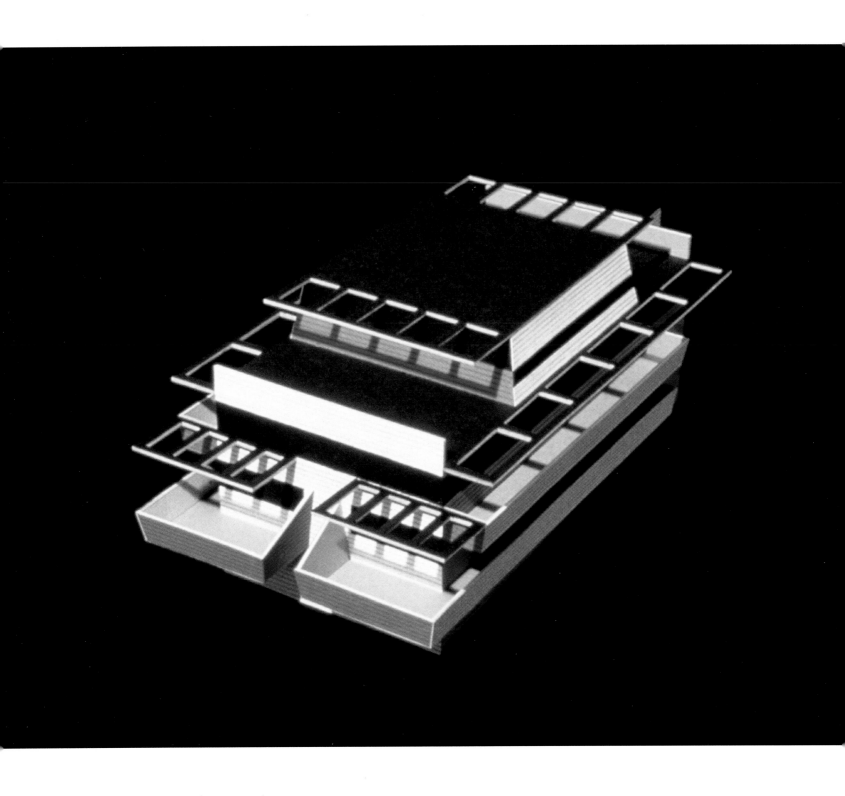

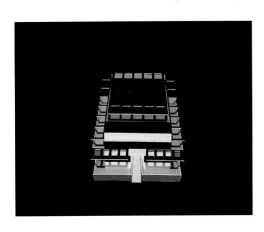

Model 1:100, competition, type "cross"

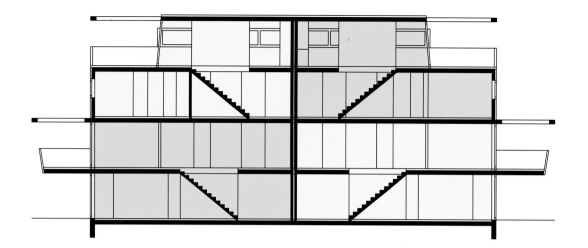

Type "parallel"

Longitudinal section

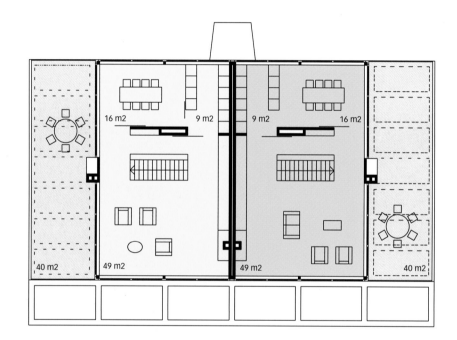

16 m2   9 m2   9 m2   16 m2

40 m2   49 m2   49 m2   40 m2

Attic

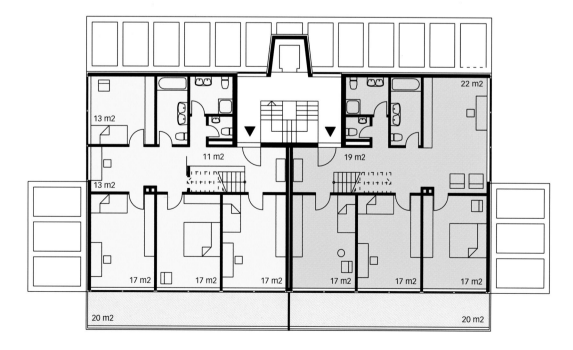

13 m2   22 m2

13 m2   11 m2   19 m2

17 m2   17 m2   17 m2   17 m2   17 m2   17 m2

20 m2   20 m2

Upper floor 1:200

90

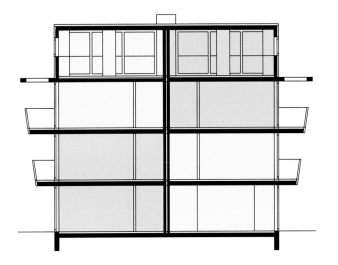

Type "crosswise"

Cross section

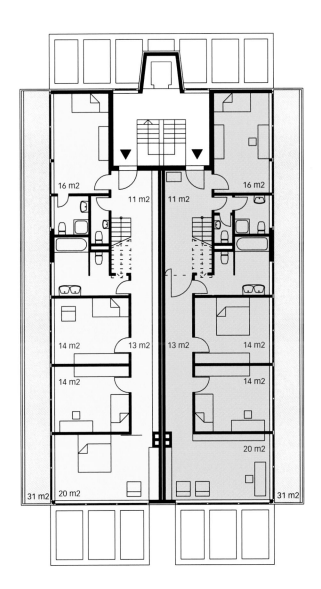

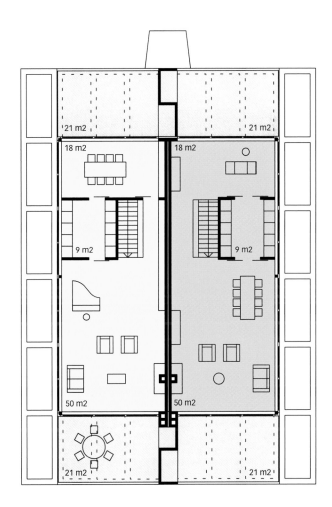

Upper floor

Attic 1:200

Kienast Vogt Partner

Remarks ▋ Site size: approx. 60 000 square feet ▋ Floors: 2 + attic ▋ Use: 0.65

TOWN VILLAS, ZURICH-WITIKON, PROJECT 1998

Competition 1998, 1st prize ▋ Client: Schindler community of heirs, Zurich ▋ Collaborators: Rainer Stotz, Hamos Meneghelli ▋
Landscape architects: Kienast Vogt Partner, Zurich

As in Herrliberg, this differentiated single-family housing development is the result of diagonally aligned and connected building volumes with varying orientations. They refer to the rural buildings of the former vineyard crosswise to the slope, and to the semidetached houses lengthwise to the slope. Similar to the houses by Alfred Roth and Marcel Breuer in Zurich Doldertal (1936), the buildings consist of two apartments and a clearly set-off attic floor. Contrary to the Herrliberg apartments, they are developed around an interior core, and the continuous balconies were replaced by pre-hung loggias. The projects in Herrliberg and Witikon further refer to the idea of the palazzine that were built in Rome by Libera and Moretti from the mid-thirties on as a sensible typology for the up-market urban apartment housing.

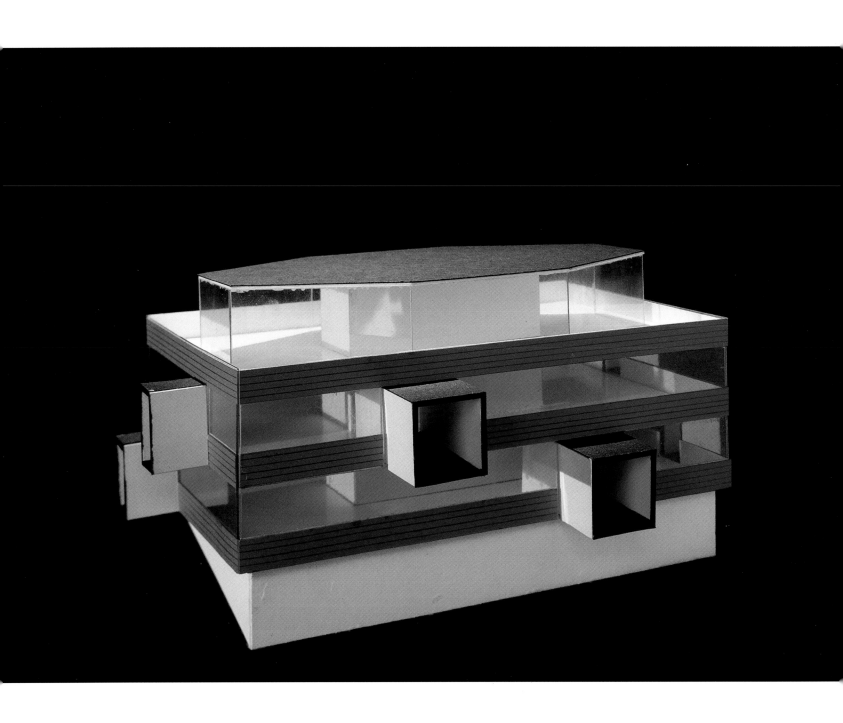

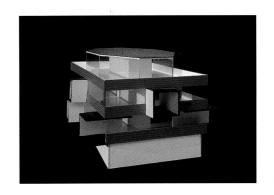

Model 1:100 competition

Type "crosswise"

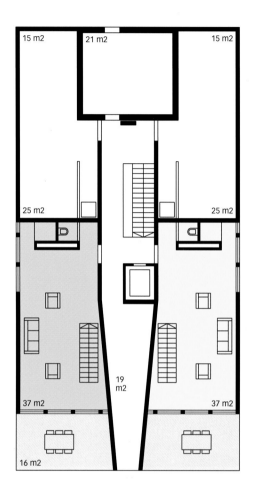

Type "parallel"

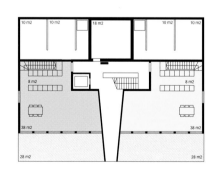

Garden level

Entrance floor

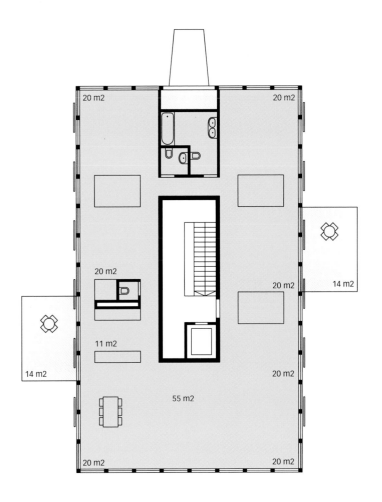

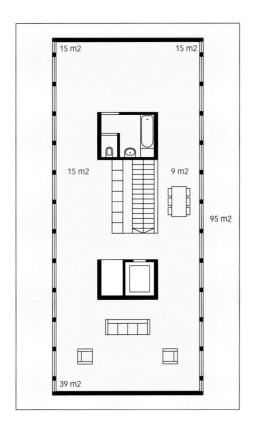

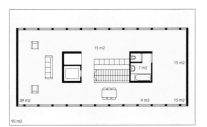

Upper floor

Attic 1:200/1:400

and the elevations appropriately investigate literal and phenomenal transparency.[11] They call out the vertical service cores and the free space vertically, overlaid with the horizontality of the semi-transparent balconies. In both schemes, the stair is treated as merely circulation; any notion of it as a social space is dropped.

Le Corbusier's pronouncement that "the problem of the house has not yet been stated" is still valid, though in its demand for investigative vigor rather than in its positivist assumptions. Once the architect chooses modification over simple invention or convention, he or she is spared what must be the unbearable burden of genius and its almost invariable consummation in either tragedy or farce while still needing to be inventive and nimble. As we see paradigmatically in these housing projects, for Marianne Burkhalter and Christian Sumi the contemporary architect has "no choice but to tread the narrow path between, on the one hand, traditional design concerns such as program, space, representation and tectonics, as well as the continual radical questioning of fundamental precepts, and, on the other, a curiosity and openness with regard to new approaches."[12] While the significance of housing is often mediated by utilitarian and economic considerations, it is precisely within its difficult, contradictory demands that Marianne Burkhalter and Christian Sumi dauntingly find sustenance, not least in the problematic correspondence between pro-

---

[11] Colin Rowe, Robert Slutzky, "Transparency: Literal and Phenomenal", *The Mathematics of the Ideal Villa and Other Essays* (Boston: 1976), Colin Rowe, Robert Slutzky, "Transparency" (Basel: 1997). See also note 12 below.

[12] Marianne Burkhalter and Christian Sumi, "Form and Profession," in *AA Files* 34 (1998): 56.

gram and form.[13] Their housing work asserts the complexities inherent in designing something quotidian, the necessity of progress and tradition, and the need to be precise without being pedantic.

---

[13] The contemporary return of program has been waged on many fronts. An entertaining and early example is Koolhaas's paeans to the Downtown Athletic Club in Delirious New York (1978), where the outrageousness of the program is contrasted with the anonymity of the form. For Koolhaas, it is this contradiction which provides the richness which is metropolitanism. The advocacy of the decorated shed by Venturi et al. (Learning from Las Vegas, 1972) can also be read in this light.

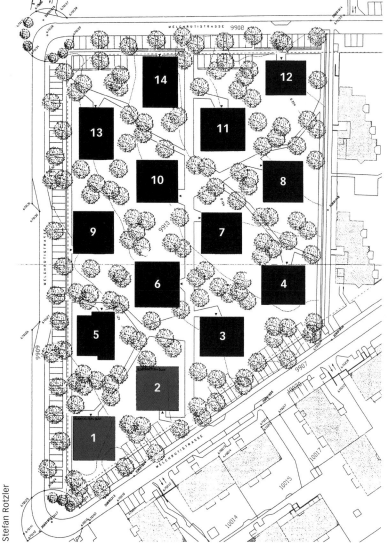

Stefan Rotzler

Remarks ▌ Site size: approx. 172 000 square feet ▌

Floors: 4 + attic ▌ Use: 0.9

The architects:

Marianne Burkhalter and Christian Sumi, Zurich (1, 2), Meinrad Morger
and Heinrich Degelo, Basel (3, 4), Jakob Steib, Zurich (5, 6),
Valentin Bearth and Andrea Deplazes, Chur (7, 8,) Sabine Hubacher
and Christoph Haerle, Zurich (9, 10), Annette Gigon and Mike Guyer,
Zurich (11, 12), Jasmin Grego and Jojo Smolenicky, Zurich (13, 14)

FULL-FLOOR APARTMENTS, WALLISELLEN, PROJECT 1997

Project management: Büro Wuest & Partner, Martin Hofer, Zurich ▌ Client: Streich AG, general contractors, Brüttisellen ▌

Collaborators: Hermann Kohler ▌ Landscape architects: Stefan Rotzler, Gockhausen

The site is characterized by the intense, overheated building development (industrial buildings, shopping centers, highways, etc.) in the agglom-
erate communities after 1945. Dispersion and loss of identity are the familiar consequences. The project attempts to counteract this development, and the urban sprawl connected with it, in an unpretentious manner: 14 cube houses of similar size designed by seven different architects
occupy the property like pairs of twins. The seven pairs were assigned to the architects by the drawing of lots.

What is interesting is the unity of house and apartment levels – that is, each apartment has a 360° view of the environment. We developed two
contrary house types or updated familiar ground plans: The standard square plan from the sixties (as, for example, in Wettswil), but now as a
free-standing unit, with interior core and elevator, bathrooms on the north side and continuous southern balcony fronting the living room; the
quarter shop is on the ground floor. And the Palladian-cross ground plan: the service rooms are integrated into the supporting cores, following
the tradition of the pochés of the Ecole des Beaux-Arts.

South façade

North façade

Façade "standard" ▌ Façade "cross" 1:200

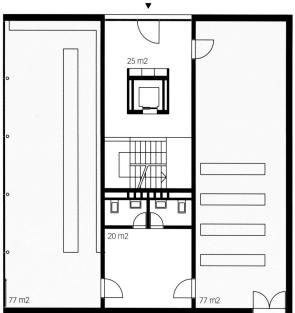

Standard ground plan

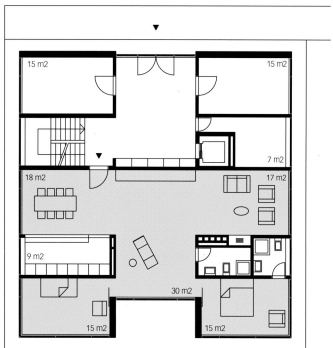

Cross-shaped ground plan

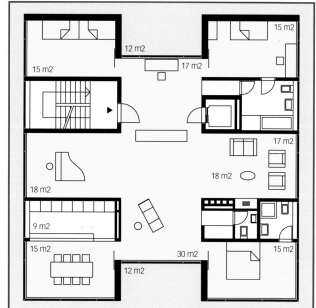

First floor

1st and 3rd upper floor

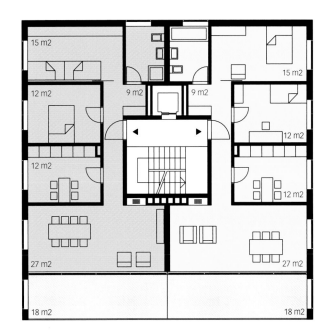

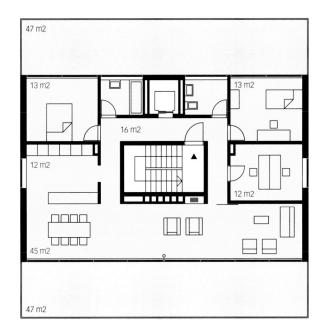

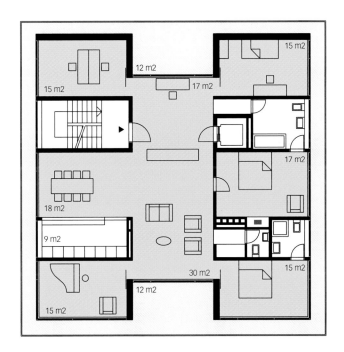

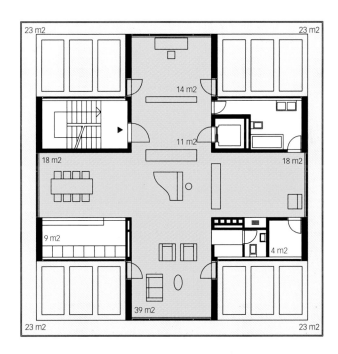

2nd upper floor   Attic 1:200

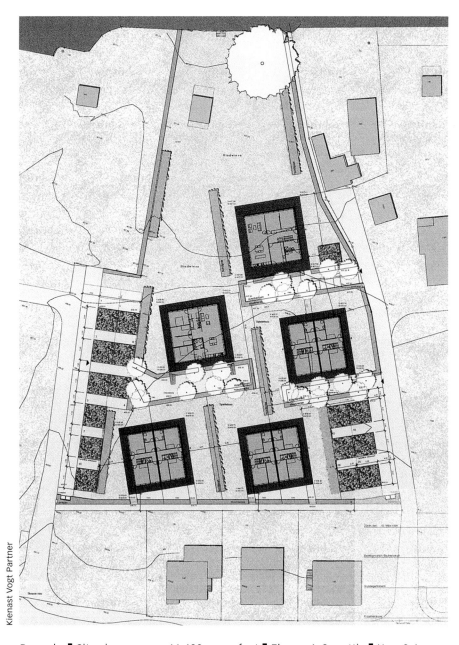

Kienast Vogt Partner

Remarks ▌ Site size: approx. 66 400 sqare feet ▌ Floors: 1–2 + attic ▌ Use: 0.4

SEMIDETACHED HOUSES, ALTENDORF, PROJECT 1999

Client: Heinr. Hatt-Haller AG, Zurich ▌ Collaborators: Claudia Murer, Barbara Ruppeiner ▌ Project Architect: Architechnic AG Regensdorf ▌ Wood Construction Engineer: Makiol + Wiederkehr, Beinwil a. See ▌ Engineer: K. Bischofberger Ingenieurbüro AG, Lachen ▌ Landscape architects: Kienast Vogt Partner, Zurich

In order to make the property tangible as a unified whole, the different programs – single-family home, townhouse and three-family home – were solved with the same basic geometric form, the square. As in Melchrüti, this creates a higher degree of unity. The houses are accessed via paved forecourts surrounded by hedges. The carports are situated directly on the two dead-end roads. The 5 houses are realized as standardized wooden constructions. The layer of beams is turned on each floor by 90 degrees. The cantilevering of the beams relieves the load moments of the span of the ceilings.

Model semidetached house 1:50

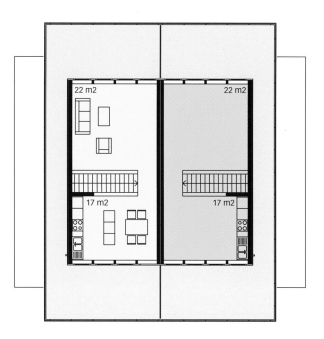

Attic

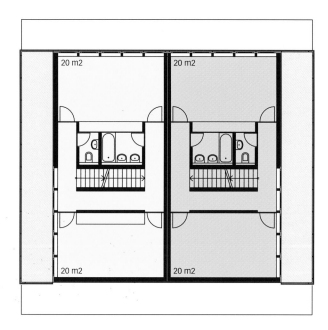

Upper floor

Semidetached house

First floor 1:200

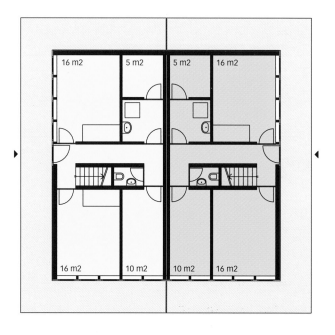

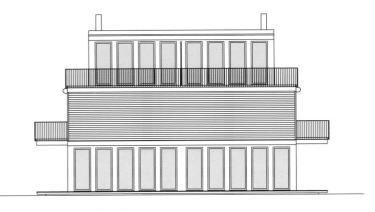

South façade

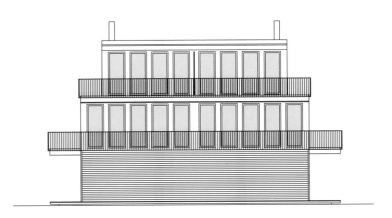

North façade

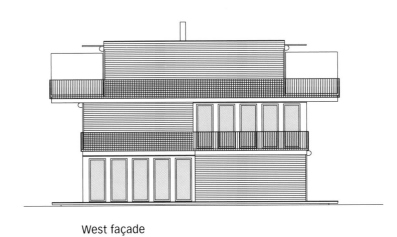

West façade

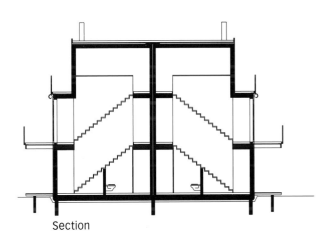

Section

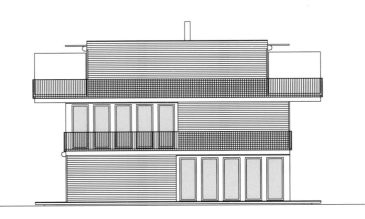

East façade 1:200

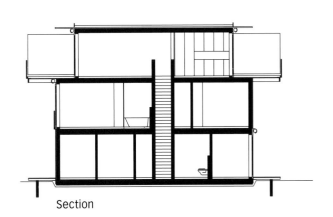

Section

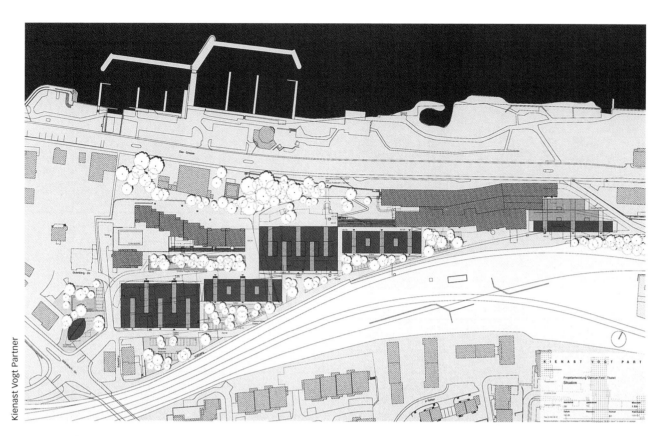

Kienast Vogt Partner

Remarks ▌ Site size: approx. 176 530 square feet ▌ Floors: 3–4 ▌ Use: 1.5

LOFT APARTMENTS, THALWIL, COMPETITION 1999

Client: Weidmann Management AG, Thalwil ▌ Collaborators: Nicole Baer, Claudia Murer,

Barbara Ruppeiner, Andrea Calanchini ▌ Landscape architects: Kienast Vogt Partner, Zurich

The 32 m-deep, three-story building volume with 29 apartments is part of the redevelopment of the former dyeworks Weidmann in Thalwil. Light-

ing and ventilation slits allow daylight to enter into the building. At the same time, they spatially expand the floor-through loft apartments and

generate the view from inside the apartments along the planted wall to the outside. The project connects the research into overly-deep building

volumes, as, for example, Le Corbusier's Unité d'habitation with a building depth of 22 m, with the experiences of condensed housing that we

have suggested for Erfurt and Berlin-Köpenick.

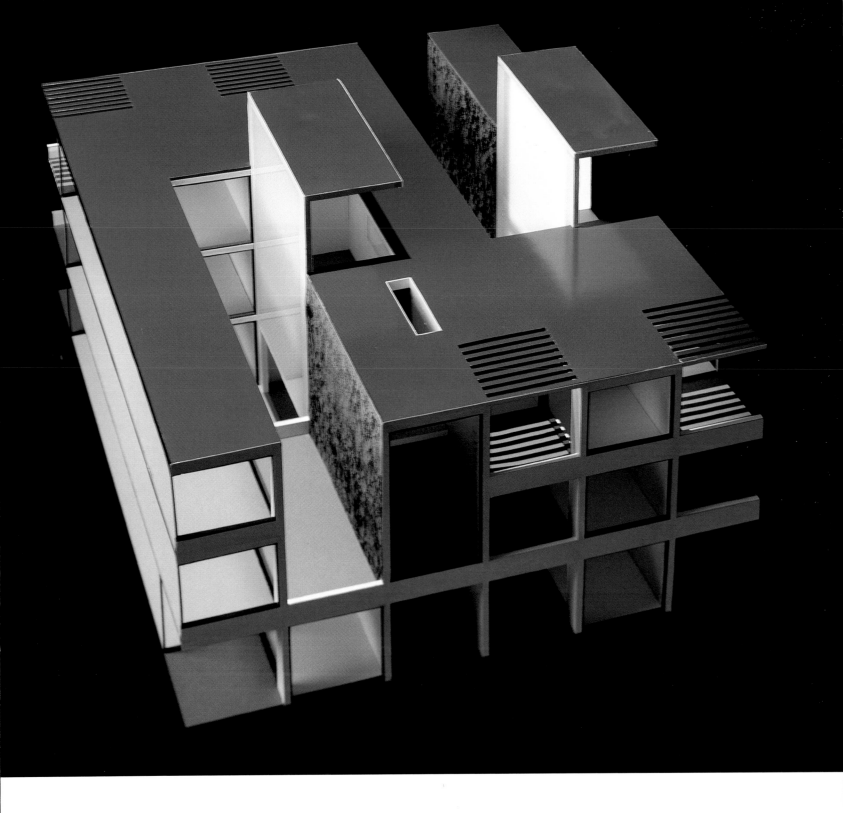

Model 1:50

14 m2   14 m2   39 m2   14 m2   21 m2   57 m2   39 m2   14 m2   21 r

69 m2   25 m2   25 m2   25 m2   25 m2   25 m2

18 m2   18 m

69 m2   18 m2   18 m2

25 m2

14 m2   14 m2   21 m2   14 m2   83 m2   39 m2   39 m2   14 m2   21 m2   14 m2   83 m2   39 m

Upper floor 1:200

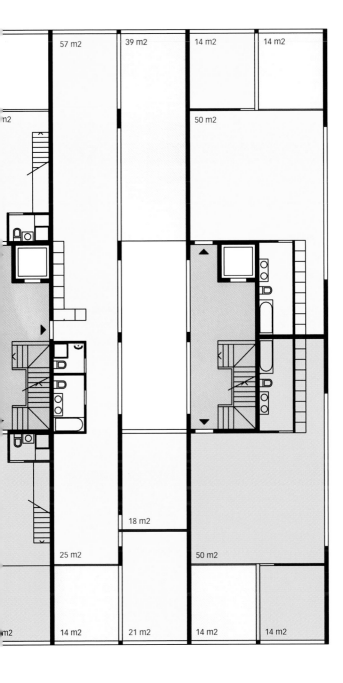

57 m2

39 m2

14 m2

14 m2

m2

50 m2

18 m2

25 m2

50 m2

m2

14 m2

21 m2

14 m2

14 m2

TIMBER – PHILOSOPHY OF THE MATERIAL

EUGENE ASSE

One of the tests conducted by the Moscow Architectural Laboratory, entitled "Presentation – Representation," involved making a precise rubbing of an existing brick wall and presenting it next to the original. The test report states: "… the original wall consists of brick, cement and plaster. Everything else is just assumption and recollection. Using this process, we have succeeded in separating pure architectural substance from the idea of [the substance] and have displayed them in different rooms …" This demonstration of material values in architecture and the demystification of architectural semantics, following years of tyranny by metaphors and allusions, seems very close to Burkhalter and Sumi's philosophy.[1]

[1] It took me almost twenty years to arrive at the demystification of architectural linguistics. Although today I am very critical of post-modern architectural philosophy, I believe that these years contributed greatly to my professional thinking.

Since the early 70s, along with my colleagues Alexander Larin and Leonid Voltchek (at the Moscow Municipal Architectural Office Mosproekt-1), I have had a strong interest in the idea of the integration of conventional signs in architectural forms. We tried, paradoxically, to combine the lessons of Venturi with the ideas of the Russian Constructivists. Such an ambiguous strategy was most likely a sort of intuitive reaction to the specific cultural and ideological conditions in the Soviet Union at that time. The new trend of international architecture could hardly be called postmodernism in a country where the modernist tradition was violently broken and the very word "modernism" was taboo. It was therefore important for us to demonstrate our conviction of a Constructivist concept of simple and functional structural form.

At the same time, we became very enthusiastic about "architecture of meaning," whose influence began penetrating through the Iron Curtain. In these terms our concept, never formulated theoretically, was based on developing meaningful form directly from the very structure and function of the building, never from applied signs or decoration. The sign and the structure were treated as an ontological whole. We were not interested in metaphorical or allusive messages, but only in signs of direct and unambiguous meaning, i.e., signs as signals. In one way, it was an attempt to interpret the suprematic visual images and constructivist typography in architectural form.

The Pharmacy in Moscow (1975/76) was built according to our design, although the construction was of a very low quality. The building, nevertheless, illustrates this approach clearly. The red cross is used in this case as an absolutely conventional sign and a very powerful simple form. At the same time, it serves not only as a billboard or decorative porch, but as a necessary functional element which encloses the entrance lobby

An important issue in their architecture is materiality. According to Paul Valery, Mallarme once said to Degas, "Verses, my dear Degas, are not made of ideas. They are made of words."[2]

An architectural interpretation of this sentence would imply that buildings, like verses, are not composed of ideas but of material facts. In these terms, the works of Burkhalter and Sumi can be considered an architecture of nouns, as opposed to the wide-spread postmodern architecture of adjectives. The realm of their creativity is not "architectural text" but the material substance of being. The material in their architecture presents its own sense and essential logic of structure and form, the architectural forms defining themselves through the material in their own typological terms. Instead of utilizing symbols or metaphors, each form unambiguously demonstrates its functional, spatial and material properties. In this way, the roofs of the Forstwerkhof manifest their "roofness," the "trunk-columns" their wooden-ness, and the "Zürichberg oval" its oval-ness.

The essence of Burkhalter and Sumi's aesthetic and ethic strategy is the direct spatial, tactile and visual experience of the form, light, texture and temperature of materials. All cultural meanings and references originate from basic perceptions rather than assumptions and recollections. This is

and the mechanical ventilation equipment. Unfortunately, of the series of buildings signs, such as dry-cleaners and laundries, bakeries, etc., designed for Moscow mass-housing developments, this is the only structure we were able to realize. Twenty years later, I founded the Architectural Laboratory, an informal group of Moscow architects, which "calls into question cultural and design truisms and appeals to immediate experience," and "attempts to evade the global architectural monopoly of a jovial indifferent postmodernism." (Burkhalter and Sumi, catalogue for the Architectural Laboratory: Moscow 1997).

[2] Paul Valery, *ob iskusstve* (About art) (Moscow: 1993): 322.

an architecture of presentation, not representation.[3] In this respect, it is not incidental that Burkhalter and Sumi use timber in many of their works. The choice of timber means much more than just a preference for one material over others; it indicates the choice of a philosophy of existence and design. In medieval English, "timber" and "house" were synonymous. The German word "Zimmer" has the same root, and both are akin to the Latin "domus". Seen in this way, the concept of timber extends from the material to the structural element and, finally, to the entire building.

The preface from The Carpenter and Joiners Assistant, published in the 1800s, reads: "The Framing of Timber for structural purposes may be regarded both as a mechanical and as a liberal art. As a mechanical art, it embraces the knowledge of the various ways of executing different works, of the process of fashioning timber, of the tools which have to be used, and the manner of handling them. As a liberal art, it includes a knowledge of geometry, of the principles of mechanics, of the nature and

---

[3] The distinction between presentation and representation is directly connected to the idea of realism in architecture, and in culture in general. As soon as presentation means the actual being (or presence) of things as they are, i.e., reality, representation deals with images of things as they could be or as they appear. In these terms, Russian culture, with its preference for literature and description, is basically a culture of representation. This element of Russian culture exerts a strong effect on contemporary Russian architecture. All the false towers, pinnacles, arches, etc., in today's Moscow indicate its complete break with existential reality. It would seem that the very idea of simplicity and clarity is completely unacceptable in this country. At the same time, we are living in an extensive float of communication that makes any exaggerations in contemporary architecture seem especially odd. The virtual streams of information traversing architectural space are neither fixed nor controlled within it. For this reason, I consider the conditions defining contemporary cultural to be "post-spatial." What an architect can do under these conditions is "not deal with superficial, permanently changing messages but with basic, elemental issues only: such as sunshine, gravity, local climate and materials, human dimensions and perceptions." See Asse, Eugene. "Posle Prostanstra" (After space), *Khudojestvennyi Zhournal* (Art journal) 16 (1997): 59.

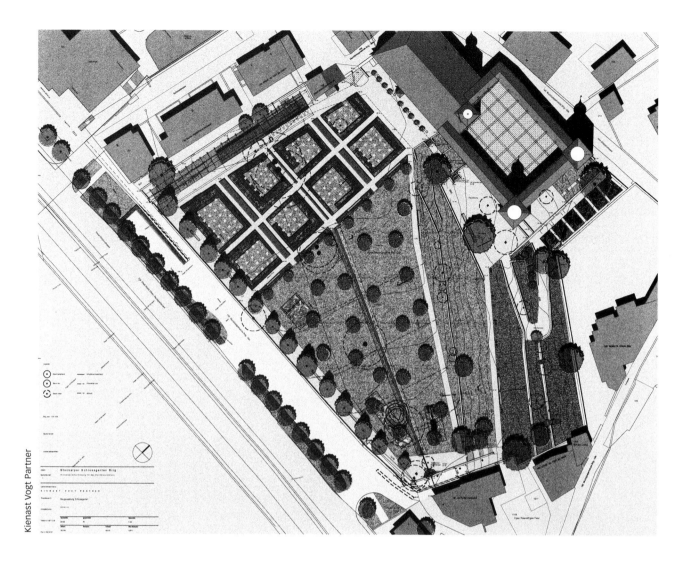

Kienast Vogt Partner

WOODEN PAVILION IN THE PARK OF STOCKALPER CASTLE, BRIG, PROJECT 1998

Client: Swiss Foundation for Stockalper Castle, Brig ▌ Collaborators: Rainer Stotz, Nicole Bär ▌ Landscape architects: Kienast Vogt Partner, Zurich

The small garden pavilion is part of the comprehensive restructuring of the park at Stockalper Castle by landscape architects Kienast Vogt Partner who won the competition. An arcade roof with climbing roses covers both the entrance ramp into the park and a small café. The theme of the oversized bench is interpreted in two ways: inside, as a "café bench," and outside, as a huge "garden bench" that is as high as the façade. We first used the "long bench" in the case of Hotel Zürichberg; we had also intended to use it in a new version for the hall of the district center Schwamendingen as a typical element of old dance halls. Distortions of scale, the creation of supra-symbols as one possibility to "place semantics immediately into the space," has fascinated us for some time. Historic examples can be found in the buildings by Frank Furness, such as the university library in Philadelphia (1887–91), renovated by the Venturis, with the over-sized chimney and the "station clock" in the reading hall, or some of Sullivan's bank buildings in the American West, with their oversized front façades reminiscent of safe locks. The pharmacy buildings by Larin and E. Asse, with the pharmacy cross, also belong in this category.

Model 1:100

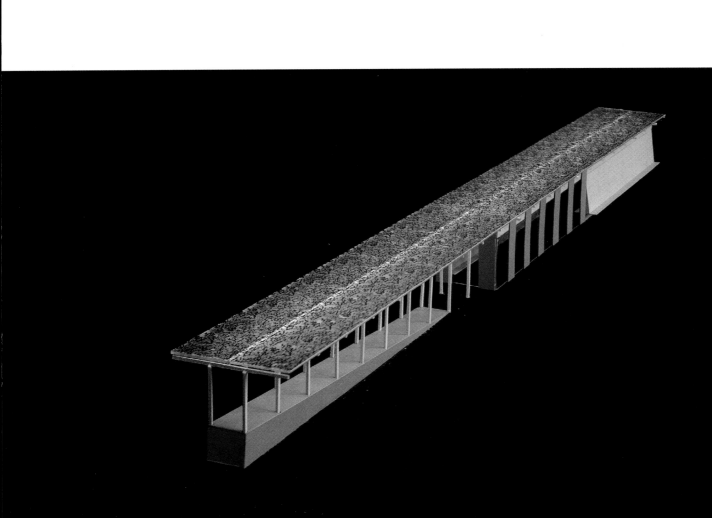

strength of the material, and its behaviour under the strains to which it is subjected."[4] In addition to these arts, of which they are unquestionably masters, Burkhalter and Sumi demonstrate in their works the fine art of timber framing, which combines traditional Swiss craftsmanship with a unique intellectual sensibility and artistic imagination.

The very special constructive and cultural qualities of timber decisively affect the principles of form-making and the entire design process. Timber is the only building material which is never liquid in any state, unlike clay, steel or concrete. Because of this property, it resists fluidity, i.e., uncertainty. It will not allow structural falsehood, but requires the very exact design of each and every junction. Timber construction is, at its base, the assembly of elements and the subsequent structural connection of one element to another. In Burkhalter and Sumi's timber detailing, even such an ordinary matter as board cladding has an almost clockwork precision. The result is a minimalist form of art.

As an organic product, timber lays the foundation for the continuing integrity of a structure. The concept of assembling a whole from separate elements is evident in all Burkhalter and Sumi's works, from the overall mass to the smaller details. And yet each element remains relatively independent and distinct. In the same way that individual boards work together to form a complete wall, the individual volumes of the Lustenau Kindergarten, for instance, join together to form an indissoluble entirety. The classic order of architecture, originally wooden, was also based on

[4] Michael Foster, ed., *The Principles of Architecture* (Oxford: 1982): 55.

the same principle of the assembly and distinction of simple forms as the whole – providing the context for a remark made by the architects during a private talk: "We are classical architects."

As the only construction material which is born, lives, and dies, wood is closely associated with the human body. Apart from its warmth and tactile merits, timber is, after all, an organically modular material. Its measure and scale are predicted, not by artist's whim, but by natural factors. This innate proportional relationship of a board or a beam to human dimensions retains the human scale in a timber building of any size. For this reason, all of Burkhalter and Sumi's constructions, despite their type, are in scale and spirit timbers of medieval meaning, i.e., houses destined for human life.

As a natural, organic and basic folk material, timber calls for simplicity. Quiet and modest, timber resists exaggeration of any kind. The simple is something which is equal to itself, and which exists in the most possible modesty without shortages or excesses.[5] As in contemporary architecture, the very idea of form becomes quite obscure; "simple" for Burkhalter and Sumi means, above all, "clear." Clarity in their works results in the exclusion of all unnecessary forms, and the reduction of necessary forms to their typological essence. They always deal with clear geometry, evident details and plain structures through the philosophy of timber. It is easy to fall into morality when appealing to a sense of the essential and simple. Fortunately, Burkhalter and Sumi escape didactics in their architecture.

[5] A. Mikhailov Heidegger, *Vmesto Vvedenia* (Instead of Introduction) (Moscow: 1993): xxvi.

West façade

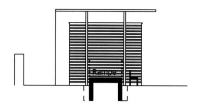

South façade

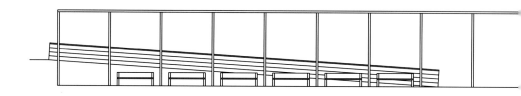

East façade

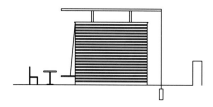

North façade

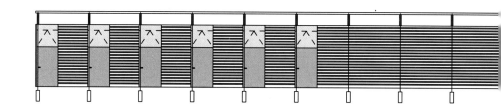

Section B-B

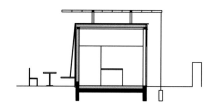

Roof elevation

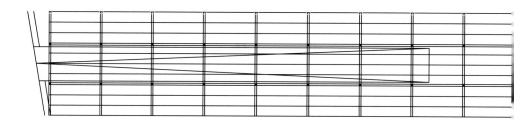

Section A-A

Ground plan

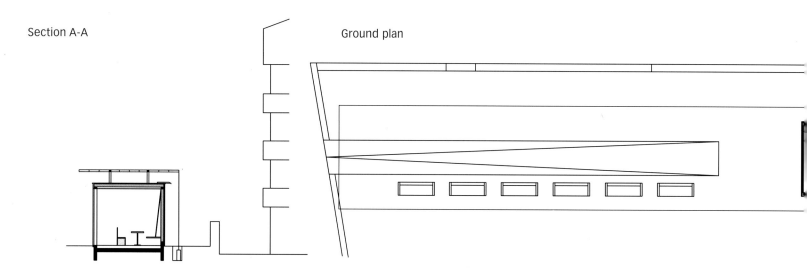

1:200

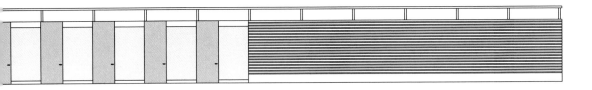

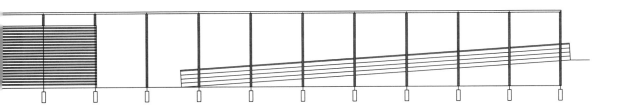

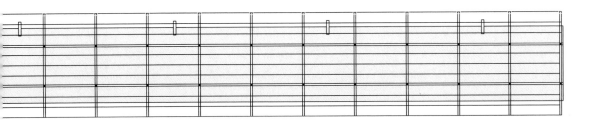

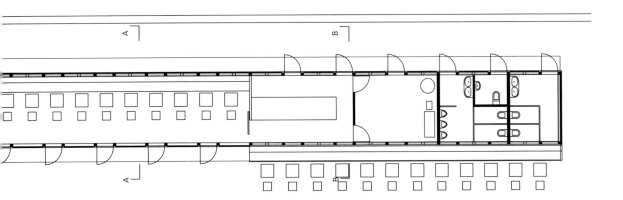

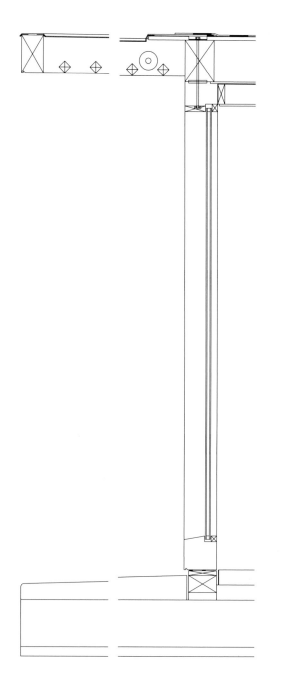

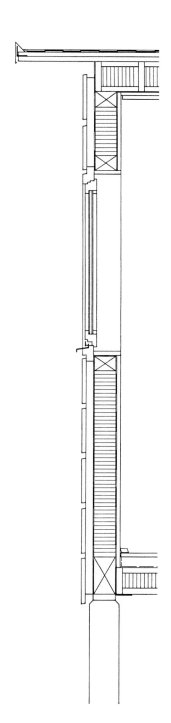

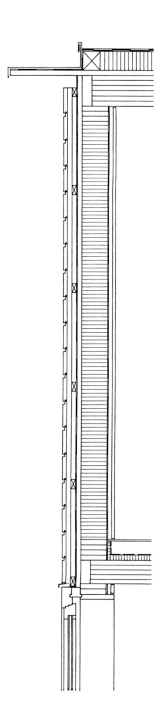

Langenberg 1:20   Forestry stations   Lustenau

They realize that architecture has lost its innocence forever, that there is no longer room for total purity in actual culture. At the same time, contemporary architecture offers such freedom of form-making that the refusal of that uncontrolled freedom in favor of clarity and intellectual discipline is the only real avant-garde strategy of today. With their joyful, vivid and extremely human architecture, Burkhalter and Sumi prove that this strategy leads to powerful and precise results. In their search for zero degree[6] based on the philosophy of material, they reach the point of positive zero.

[6] Martin Steinmann, "The Presence of Things in Construction, Intention, Detail," (Zurich: 1994): 24.

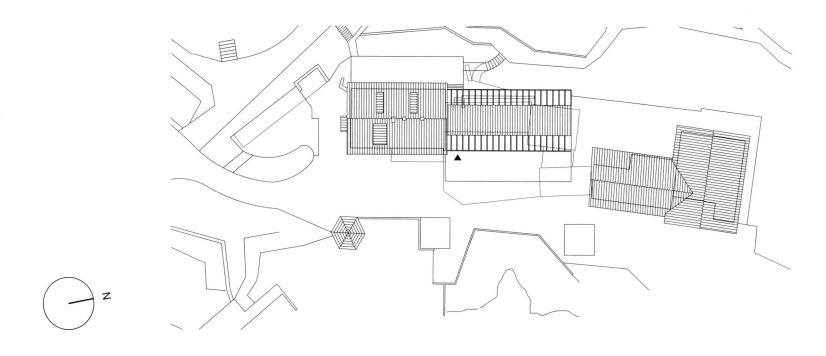

WOODEN PAVILION FOR THE GAME PARK LANGENBERG, LANGNAU AM ALBIS, 1998

Client: Building Department of the City of Zurich ▌Collaborators: Michael Fischer ▌Project architects: Burkhalter und Sumi Architekten,

represented by: GMS Partner AG, Zurich ▌Engineers: Stucki Hofacker + Partner AG, Zurich, Mr. Hofacker /SHNZ Cham, Mr. Krebs

The relocation of the bear cage has altered the situation of the existing 1944 restaurant by the municipal architect, A. H. Steiner. The location was reversed and the main action was moved from the front to the rear. The new wooden pavilion, together with the old barn which is to be converted into an information and training center at a later date, forms the new core of the game park. The strongly cantilevered parapet serves as a protection from the sun, signals publicity, and invites visitors to enter the pavilion. Extensive glazing and doors painted red characterize the rhythm of the building. Ventilation is effected via openings in the doors and the simple ventilation devices on the roof. The roof is slightly slanted; rainwater is drained away by sheet-metal gutters.

Views with the existing building by A.H. Steiner

Interior

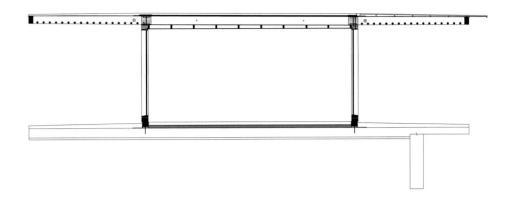

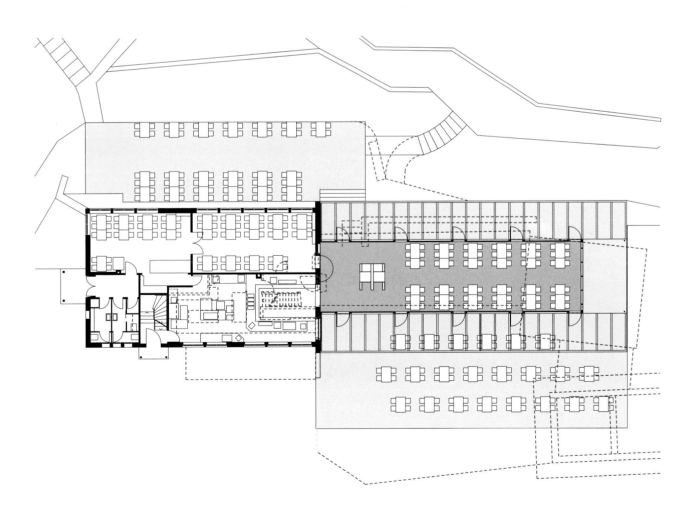

Cross section 1:100 ▐ Ground plan 1:300

View with Albis in the background

Details of cantilevered canopy

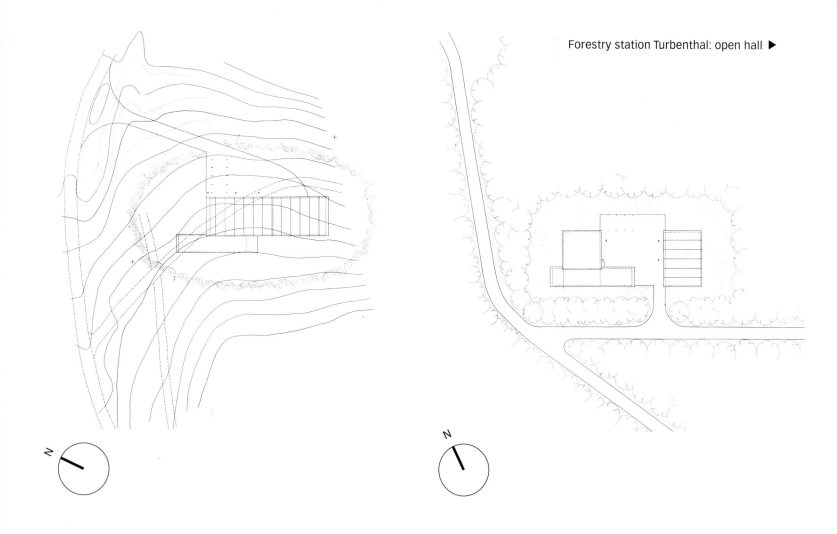

FORESTRY STATION, TURBENTHAL, 1993/FORESTRY STATION, RHEINAU, 1994

Forestry Station, Turbenthal ▌ Client: Building Department of the Canton of Zurich ▌ Collaborators: Marianne Dutli, Andrea Bassi ▌
Project Architects: Arthur Schlatter, Wernetshausen ▌ Engineers: Stucki Hofacker + Partner AG, Zurich, Mr. Hofacker/SHNZ Cham, Mr. Krebs

Forestry Station, Rheinau ▌ Client: Building Department of the Canton of Zurich ▌ Collaborators: Sybille Bucher, Andrea Bassi ▌
Project Architects: Arthur Schlatter, Wernetshausen ▌ Engineers: Stucki Hofacker + Partner AG, Zurich, Mr. Hofacker/SHNZ Cham, Mr. Krebs

The basis of the project is a modular system whose parts can be put together according to the location and wishes of the users. It consists of three parts: the administration, the garage and the open hall. In Turbenthal, the garage and hall form one building volume and the administration is pushed up against it. The two building volumes are placed parallel to the mountain ridges and, due to the varying roof silhouettes, become wedged into the ravine-like grounds. The forest ground runs below the large roof of the open hall as a kind of graveled surface. In Rheinau, the garage and the administration are separated from the open hall. They form a yard-like outdoor space and solidify the edge of the existing forest clearing. As in Turbenthal, the grounds are only covered with gravel.

Forestry station Turbenthal 1:300 ∎ Exterior view and details ▶

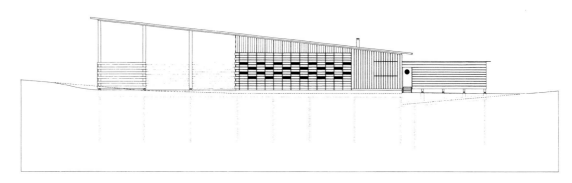

East façade

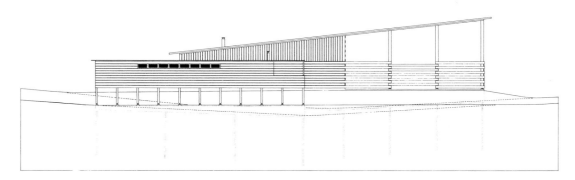

West façade

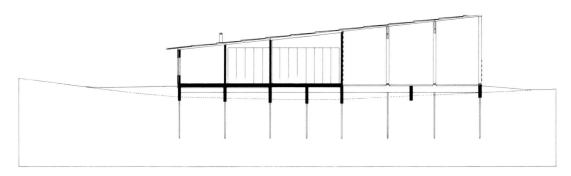

Section

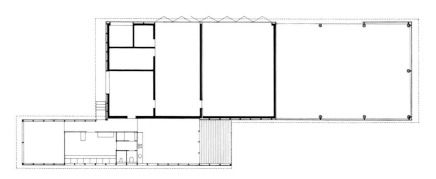

Ground plan 1:300

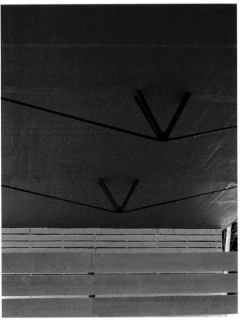

Forestry station Turbenthal: exterior view

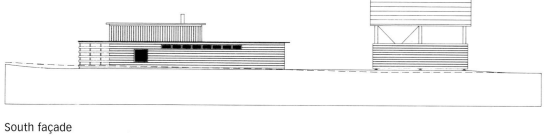

South façade

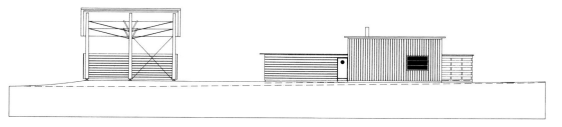

North façade

◀ Forestry station Rheinau: Interior with veranda ▮ Exterior views

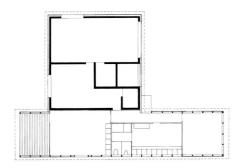 

Ground plan 1:300

Forestry station Rheinau: overall view

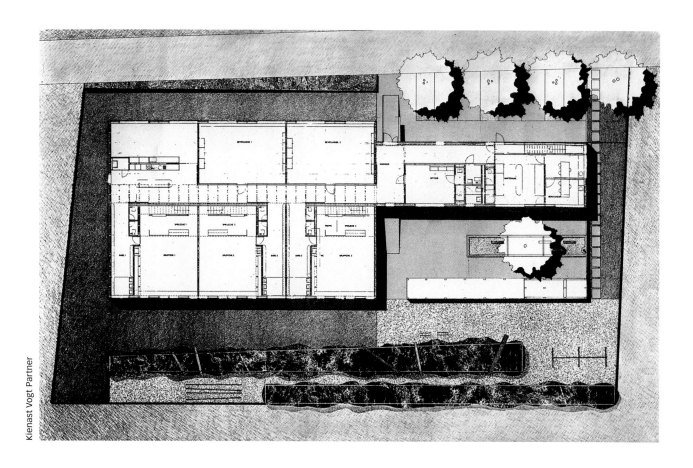

N

Kienast Vogt Partner

KINDERGARTEN AM SCHLATT, LUSTENAU, AUSTRIA, 1994

Competition, two phases, 1989, 1st prize ▌ Client: Municipality of Lustenau, Austria ▌ Collaborators: Andrea Bassi ▌

Project Architects: Lothar Huber, Lustenau ▌ Engineer: Ingo Gehrer, Höchst ▌ Landscape architects: Kienast Vogt Partner, Zurich

The new kindergarten building is based on simple cubes, similar to children's building blocks. The infant station with the employee apartments above and the three group rooms of the kindergarten are arranged diagonally and generate two zones: the ancillary rooms of the kindergarten in the northeast, and the playground with a pergola in the southeast. On the upper floor, the figure generating the design becomes visible: a stocky, angular, infinite loop in the shape of a figure eight. The perception of the building volume oscillates between a divided whole and a whole consisting of joined parts. A pure red – the color of a child's toy – was used for the volumes; white was used for the receding corners in order to demarcate the building as a public institution amidst the diffuse, ill-defined surroundings. Red and white are the colors of building sites and thus of building and joining as such, which again enhances the building-block character.

Exterior views

South façade with playground

Gallery

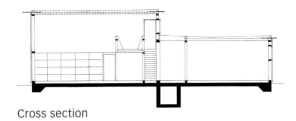

Cross section

Longitudinal section

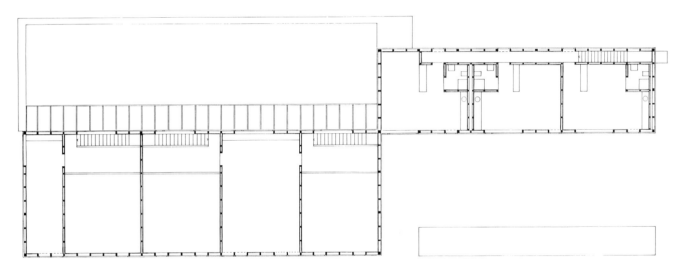

Upper floor

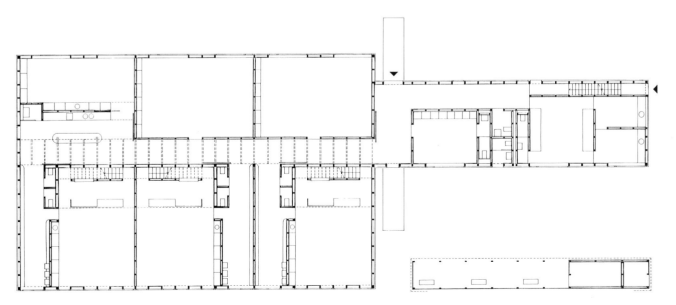

First floor 1:300

145

◀ Wardrobe access with "sliding gate" ∎ Exercise room

CONVERSIONS AND REUTILIZATIONS – CHANGING FACES

DETLEF MERTINS

During the past decade, Swiss architecture has resurfaced as a force in contemporary practice with a proliferation of new works that transfigure the modernist tradition from within. The mid-century quest for a new self-generated normativeness has quietly given way to a diversity of practices producing singular, even artistic, projects. Among the most remarkable and arresting of these, the work of Burkhalter and Sumi combines austere rationality with sensuous excess and phantasmatic theatricality. Pushing beyond the limits of cognition and order, which modernist purists had sought to delineate and enforce, their buildings mobilize the tropes of self-referential form and the geometries of tectonic self-disclosure to stage encounters with alterity and complexity. As was the case with the kind of "neue Sachlichkeit" of the 1920s that Franz Roh described in terms of magic realism,[1] Burkhalter and Sumi point to the Other as palpable within every architectonic image, yet fugitive, multiple and divergent. The renovation projects of Burkhalter and Sumi provide concentrated demonstrations of this transfiguration of modernism, for which the act of renovation itself has become paradigmatic. Rather than starting each time as if from the beginning, these works are consistently sited within

---

[1] See Franz Roh, *Nachexpressionismus: Magischer Realismus: Probleme der neuesten europäischen Malerei* (Leipzig: Klinkhardt und Biermann, 1925). For a more extended treatment of the relationship between Roh's conception of magic realism and the sustained dualities of architecture in the 1990s, see Detlef Mertins, "Open Contours and Other Autonomies," catalogue essay in *Monolithic Architecture*, ed., Rodolpho Machado and Rodolphe El Khoury (Pittsburg: The Heinz Architectural Center, The Carnegie Museum of Art, and Munich: 1995): 36–61.

the already given worlds of architecture – of buildings and sites, techniques and traditions, discourses and performative matrixes. These givens are redeployed to produce figures of vibrant optical and mysterious resonance, bringing the observer to the brink of the unknown, to a threshold from which to intuit, if not actually see beyond.[2] It can hardly be accidental that some of the most powerful images of their work are views from inside looking out toward nature, the same nature from which the materials, geometries and patterns of the buildings are drawn. These surreal images are emblematic of the play of similarity and difference that is staged in various ways by many of their projects.[3]

In order to make two historic houses in Kaiserstuhl suitable for contemporary uses, the architects inserted a set of new discrete elements into the existing shells – new kitchens and bathrooms, stairwells and corridors – intervening only where the condition of the buildings made it unavoidable. While woven discretely into the existing fabric, these new elements assert themselves as objects with discrete architectonic identities, mini-

[2] While I have argued that, within modernism, the work of Mies van der Rohe had a similar effect in relation to the given technologies and building types of his time – theorized in the first instance as residing outside architecture – here I would say that the work of Burkhalter and Sumi transfigures what is already given in architecture. See Detlef Mertins, "Mies's Skyscraper Project: Towards the Redemption of Technical Structure," *The Presence of Mies*, ed. Detlef Mertins (New York: 1994): 49–67.

[3] Writing in 1933, Walter Benjamin put forward a provocative theory of mimesis as the capacity to produce similarities with the Other. He suggested that a child playing at being a windmill or a horse or a shopkeeper was exemplary of this production of similarities, which in ancient times had been performed by dances. In the modern world, this faculty remained active but was mediated by language and other forms of representation, including technologies of reproduction such as photography, which limited its appearance to momentary flashes. A most compelling reworking of this theme is provided in Michael Taussig, *Mimesis and Alterity: A Particular History of the Senses* (New York: 1993).

For a consideration of Benjamin's mimesis in relation to architecture, see Detlef Mertins, "Walter Benjamin's Glimpses of the Unconscious: New Architecture and New Optics," *History of Photography* 22, no. 2 (Summer 1998): 116–126.

malist forms capable of generating powerful spatial effects. By introducing divergences of form, material and character, these alterations render the buildings' identities more complex, multiple and unstable. This proliferation of abstracted particles of matter produces new kinds of perceptions and experiences, employing the spatiality of the modernist open plan while tempering its homogeneity and universalist ambition with another kind of openness – accepting of contingency, incompletion, heterogeneity and contestation.

Similarly, the proposed renovation of the EMPA in Dübendorf extends the central volume of the building vertically and transforms the original open frame into an anthracite-colored block rising up from within, like an alien body. Deviating from the systematic coherence of the original structure, the new body of the building becomes less a unified whole than a composite assemblage of parts. Its gestalt is fraught with formal tensions between vertical and horizontal, planes and volumes, integration and disintegration. Still linked to the categories of Gestalt psychology, which underpinned many conceptions of modern form, these oppositions are, in the architect's work, no longer resolved into harmonies or states of equilibrium, but rather are played out as unresolved binary logics. Chaos resurfaces here within the regime of order – a gentler chaos than the one so feared in modernist discourse, a horizon of difference opened up in the gaps, shadows and slippages that sustain a buoyant instability.[4]

[4] The tensions and instabilities sustained in assemblages were integral to the idea that a new kind of image had emerged in the wake of cubism. Adolf Behne called it a "constructed image" and suggested that, with it, the model of unity through relations replaced earlier models of whole-

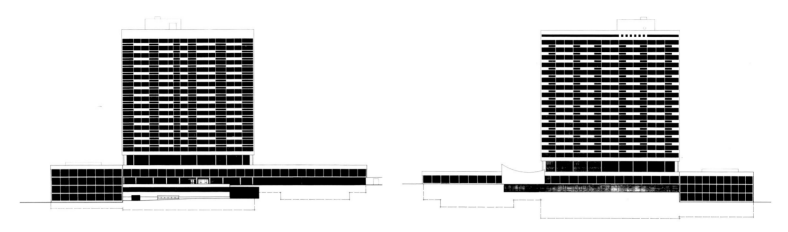

Before

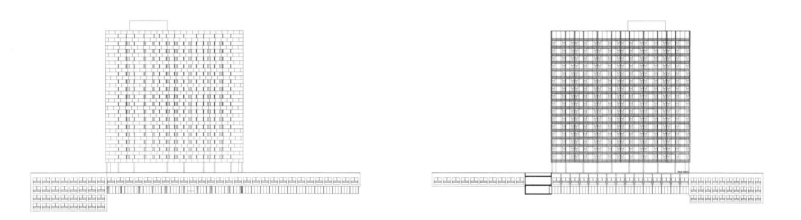

After (version no. 2)

RENOVATION OF THE FAÇADE OF THE CITY HOSPITAL TRIEMLI, ZURICH, STUDIES 1989, 1991 AND 1996

Client: Department of building inspectors of the city of Zurich, Zurich ▌ Engineer: Henauer AG, Zurich

The Triemli Hospital in Zurich by architects Schindler, Spitznagel, Burkard is a very striking sixties building characterized by a reception area from the oeuvre of late-Le Corbusier, as well as by the Brazilian architects, Lucio Costa, Oscar Niemeyer and Alfonso Reidy. The north and south façade have been unified through a space-containing façade – a kind of "sun-breaker." The flat-roofed structure and the slab building exist in a balanced relationship. The prefabricated concrete elements of this sun-breaker had been irreparably damaged for some time and needed to be replaced. Over the course of seven years, we worked out several different designs. In the first proposals, the various locations and functions of the north and south façades (patient rooms in the south and laboratories in the north) were differentiated by way of diverse façade layers. The most recent proposal reunites the north and south sides to an even greater extent. On the south side, solar panels (expected performance 200 kW) have been suggested for the last two proposals; they would function simultaneously as sun blinds.

Another set of projects operate not within but upon the surfaces of existing buildings, the very surfaces whose capacity for direct expression provided an index for gauging the self-discipline of autonomous form. The series of proposals for renovating the exterior of the Triemli Hospital in Zurich explores ways to transform the uniform plastic mass into a composite figure, more assembled and clad than shaped and formed. The original bris-soleil of monochrome precast concrete is replaced by overlapping horizontal and vertical screens in varied colors and patterns. The new layers generate a more animate, ethereal and teasing transparency than the original, which remained classical and static despite its syncopated pattern. Dark cladding of the side walls emphasizes the differences between the building's surfaces, rendering its character as whole less unified and resolved. The renovation of an apartment building in Dettenbühl similarly set out to redress not only the deterioration of the enclosure and the spatial limitations of the apartments, but also the building's image. By adding new balconies as a continuous layer in front of the existing west façade, the architects were able to capture the space of the original corner balconies for the interior and create a more generous and ambiguous zone between inside and outside – providing spatial extension, panoramic views and sun protection. Instead of the original alternation of solid and void, frontality and diagonality, new windows and doors

ness that relied on composition. Yve-Alain Bois provides an illuminating analysis of cubism's "open construction" in Yve-Alain Bois, "Kahnweiler's Lesson," Painting as Model (Cambridge, Mass.: 1990): 65–97. For a brief history of the transposition of this new form from the visual arts into architecture, see Detlef Mertins, "Anything But Literal: Sigfried Giedion and the Reception of Cubism in Germany," Architecture and Cubism, ed. Eve Blau and Nancy J. Troy (Cambridge, Mass. and Montreal: Canadian Centre for Architecture: 1997): 219–251.

dissolve the surface entirely, while a lattice of wooden planks provides a permeable, yet assertive and theatrical screen. The architects themselves describe this detached screen as a mask, alluding to games of concealment and disguise that earlier generations of modernists had eschewed.

In reiterating Swiss traditions of construction – modern as well as vernacular, in wood as in other materials – Burkhalter and Sumi remain true to the rationalist tradition while reconnecting its interrogation of artistic means with ambitions that are once again more poetic than simply cognitive. Their montagist mode of composition, informed by an understanding of the properties of materials and contemporary methods of production, serves to exaggerate the gaps between things, emphasize the assembly of discrete elements over plasticity and uniformity, and heighten contrasts. While resistant to singular or definitive readings, their projects nevertheless create an overall impression that is strong and graphic, capable of arresting the eye and giving the observer pause. Momentarily interrupting the perceptual field of everyday life, they produce a state of suspension in which divergence hovers as an expectant potentiality.

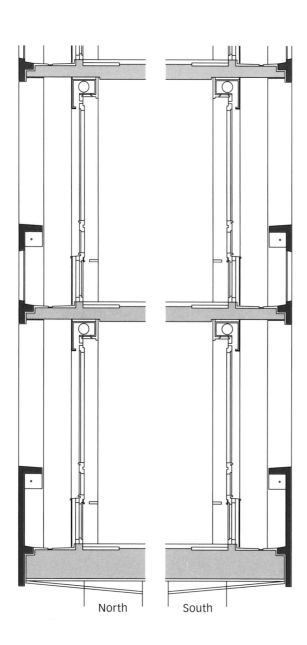

North | South

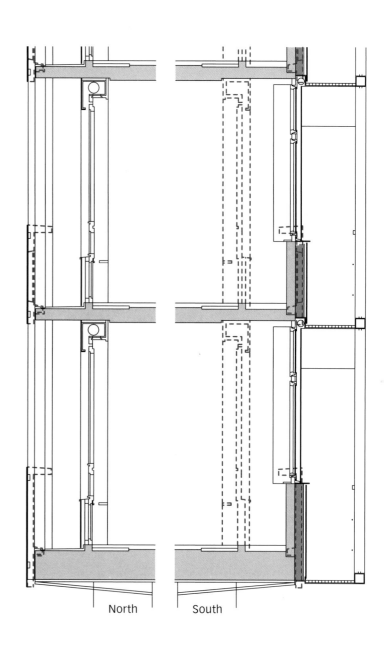

North | South

Series of sections 1:50

Current situation: the curtain concrete parapets and rocker columns show irreparable damage and have to be replaced.

Version no. 1 (1989)

South façade: extension of the rooms by the depth of the sun-breaker, addition of a new sun-breaker. North façade: replacement of the concrete elements with Eternit parapets.

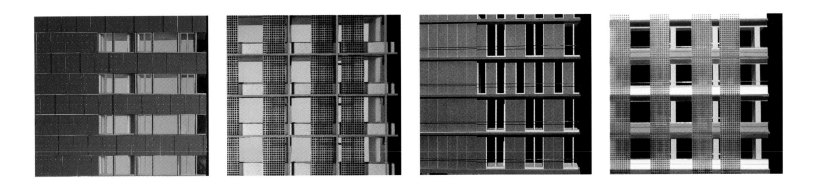

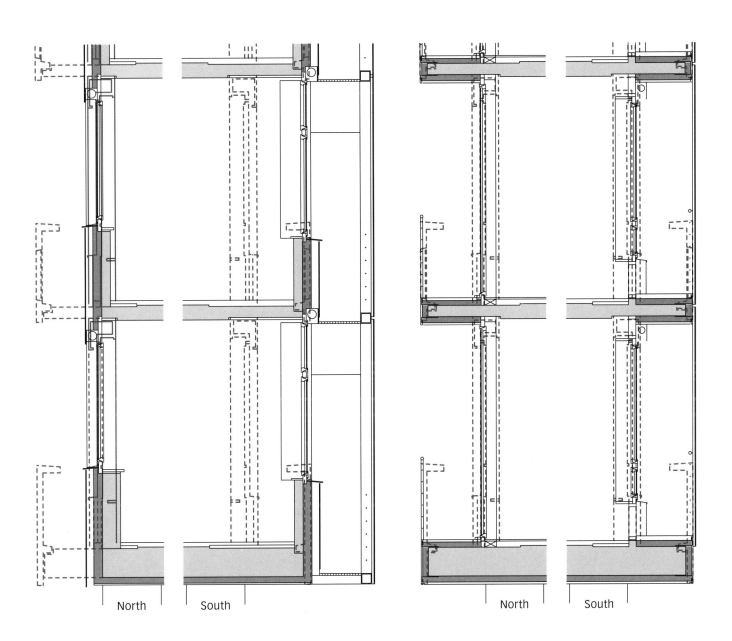

North | South

North | South

Version no. 2 (1991)

South façade: like version no. 1, but solar panels would be used instead of the wire nets. North façade: removal of the sun-breaker and addition of an entirely new facing.

Version no. 3 (1996)

South façade: preservation of the current room size, replacement of the concrete elements with solar panels and new wooden windows. North façade: like version no. 1, but with new windows and slat railing.

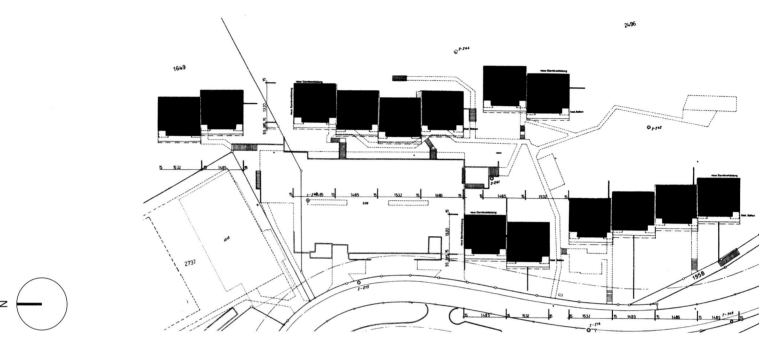

RENOVATION OF THE FAÇADE OF THE DETTENBÜHL DEVELOPMENT, WETTSWIL, 1996

Competition 1995, 1st prize ▌ Client: Building Cooperative Rotach, Zurich ▌ Collaborators: Robert Albertin ▌

Project architects: Burkhalter und Sumi Architekten, represented by: GMS Partner, Zurich ▌ Engineer: Kamm und Stähli, Wettswil ▌

Landscape architects: Kienast Vogt Partner, Zurich

The necessary replacement of the heat insulation in the development built in 1970 by architects Felix Rebmann, Maria Anderegg and Hermann Preisig offers the opportunity to enlarge the small kitchens and to essentially reorganize the interior/exterior relationship of the apartments on the west side. At the same time, the outdoor spaces are restructured. The small, dark balconies off the kitchens on the west façade are integrated and become part of the kitchen. The strip windows in the living rooms are replaced by floor-to-ceiling sliding doors, and the façade is extended forward as a whole. This creates an unbroken stretch of balcony that serves to visually expand the interior and opens up a panoramic view of the landscape. It also provides protection from the sun and creates additional storage space for the apartments. The badly insulated, plastered façades on the north, east and south sides were insulated from the outside and faced with Eternit panels. The coloration of the head and longitudinal façades are intentionally differentiated – anthracite gray and Swedish red – in order to enhance the staggered arrangement of the building volumes as an essential characteristic of this development.

Model west façade 1:50

Before

After

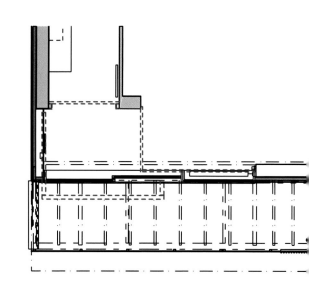

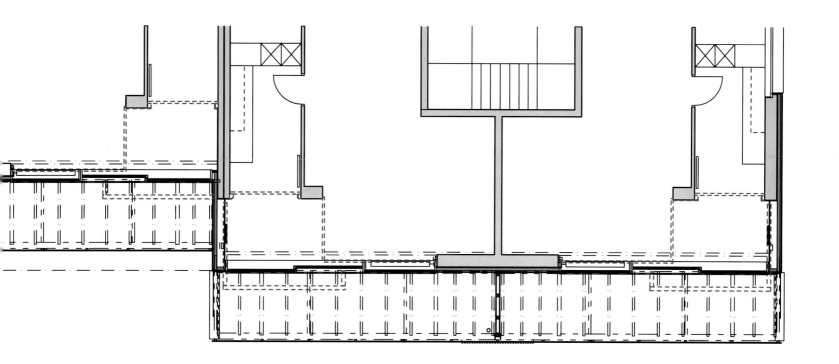

Before

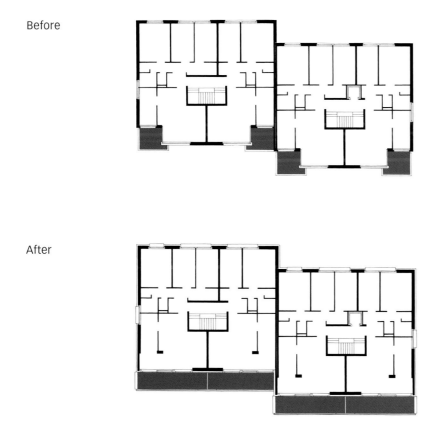

After

◀ Interior view with balcony ▮ Ground plans 1:100 and 1:400

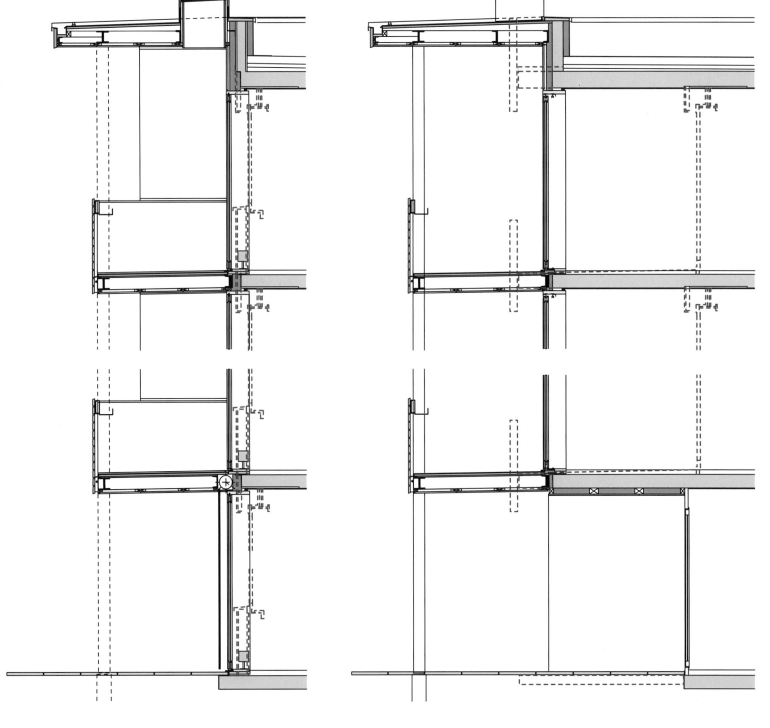

East and west façade

East and west façade

West façade

1 Ceramics building

2 Metal hall

3 Construction hall

4 Plastics testing building

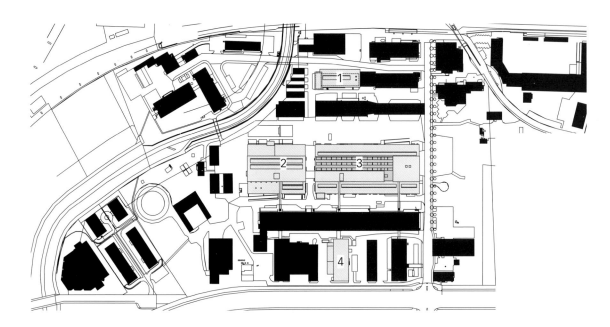

Model 1:200 ▶

RENOVATION FAÇADE EMPA, DÜBENDORF, 1999

Competition 1995, 1st prize ▮ Client: Research Center Dübendorf, former Department of Federal Buildings ▮

Collaborators: Jürg Schmid, Volker Lubnow, Hermann Kohler ▮ Project architect: Burkhalter und Sumi Architekten, represented

by GMS Partner AG, Zurich ▮ Engineers: Zimmermann + Volkert, Dübendorf/Stucki Hofacker + Partner AG Zurich,

Mr. Hofacker/SHNZ Cham, Mr. Krebs ▮ Landscape architects: Kienast Vogt Partner, Zurich

The buildings of the Eidgenössische Materialprüfungsanstalt (federal materials testing complex), or EMPA, that were erected between 1959 and 1962 by the architect Forrer, fall into the category of high-level industrial and laboratory architecture – architecture which has always been a relevant building task in Switzerland, a country that processes a vast amount of raw material. Some examples of this are the buildings by Salvisberg und Rohn for La Roche in Basel, or those by Dubois und Eschenmoser for the Saurer works in Arbon.

Construction hall before

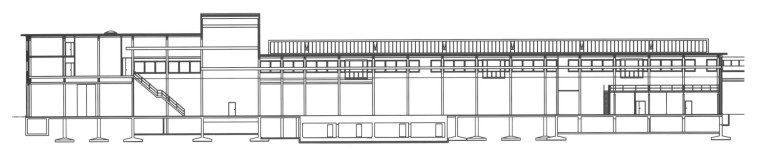

Construction hall after (with heightening)

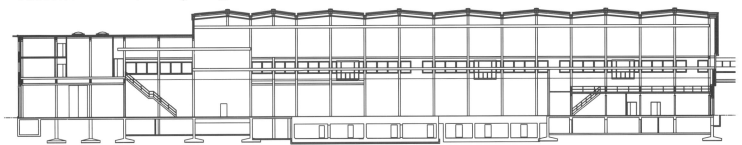

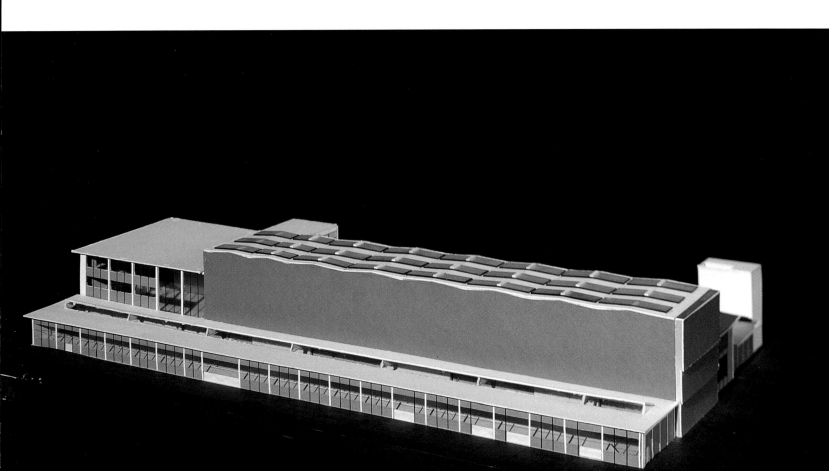

We formulated five items for the design procedure:

1. Requirements and performance ability of the existing building substance must be clarified for each case. This means that no exaggerated demands should be placed on the existing building substance.

2. Structure and extension must be differentiated, and the various lifetimes of the individual building sections have to be taken into consideration.

3. The relationship between windows and closed façade sections must be precisely checked with respect to the insulation value and, if necessary, changed (closing up of large glazed surfaces).

4. Any possible relocation of use and structural condensations or increases in height are sensible alternatives to new buildings.

5. The separate, typologically differentiated buildings by Forrer must be integrated into the overall development of the area. Architectural continuities and breaks must be carefully harmonized. The visual orientation and integral landscaping plan continue to provide the area with an inner cohesion.

For the realization of the five points and the materialization of the building shell, we developed the following four guidelines based on the materials that had already been used:

1. Roofs: The expression of the eaves is to be preserved (replacement of the copper sheet with copper-titanium-zinc sheets). This means that any increase in the height of the heat insulation is to be clearly set back from the roof edge.

2. Façades: Instead of the corrugated Eternit that is no longer available today, corrugated copper-titanium-zinc sheet will be used.

3. Openings: These have been classified and standardized by us as follows:

   gates with copper-titanium-zinc facings and "portholes" with wooden rings

   glass doors with the EMPA logo and large wooden handles

   industrial glazing for the halls

   wood and aluminum windows with ventilation wings for the offices

   new large-scale shed glazing.

4. Colors: the various shades of gray, the light yellow on the exterior and the two shades of blue inside the buildings, together with the colors of the materials' surfaces – the warm red of the brick, the metallic glimmer of the steel parts, etc. – result in a typical fifties color palette, which offers itself as a point of orientation for the coloration.

Construction hall: Models hall roof 1:50/1:10

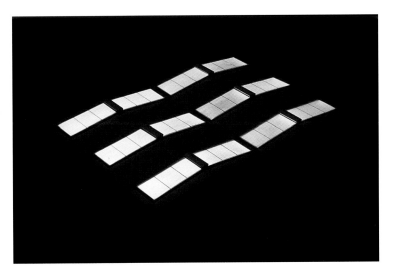
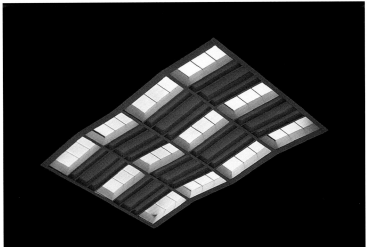

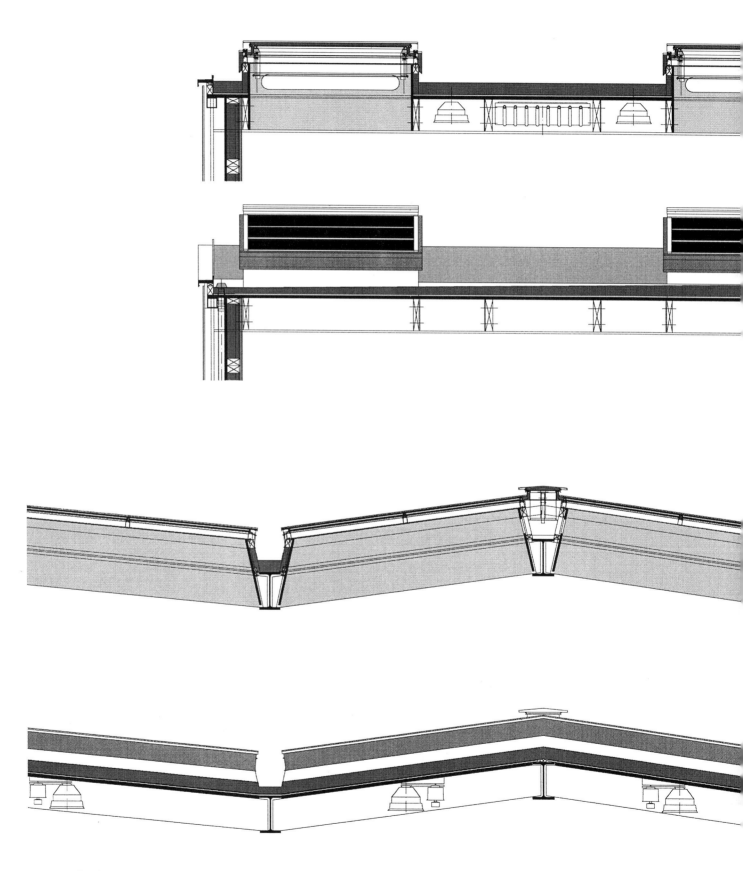

Construction hall: longitudinal and cross sections hall roof 1: 50

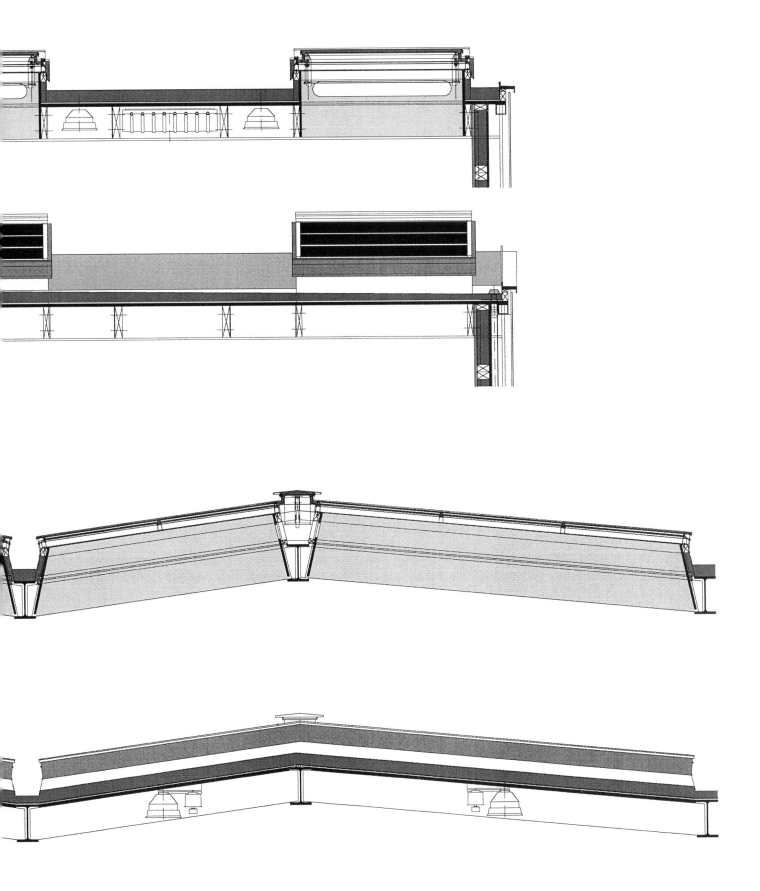

New entrance administrative building

Metal hall: new gate façade

175

Ceramics building: interiors and elevations

Before   After

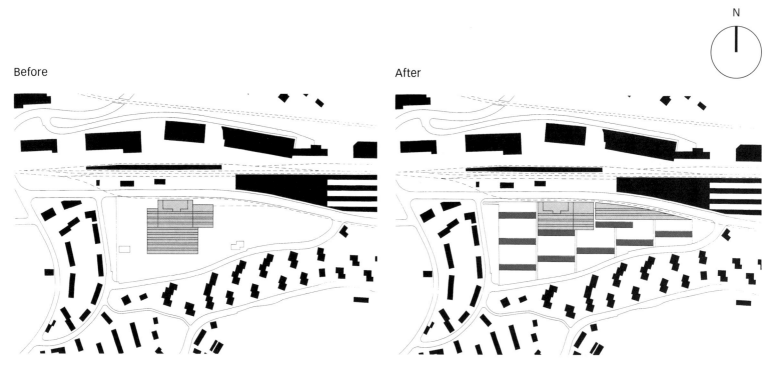

Remarks ▮ Site size: approx. 342 000 square feet ▮ Floors: 4 ▮ Use: 0.9

REUTILIZATION OF THE INDUSTRIAL AREA OF SCHINDLER, ST. GALLEN-HAGGEN, 1994 COMPETITION 1ST PRIZE

The manufacturing site of Schindler – a several-story-high complex from 1946 that include a number of shed halls that were erected at a later time – was abandoned during the eighties and finally sold. Some of the buildings are still in use today; the rest of the site has been rezoned for residential use. The proposed development pattern, with slab houses, forms a casual sequence of yard-like outdoor spaces. Part of the existing shed hall is integrated into the multi-story factory building to form the lower northern termination of the complex. A sequence of wedge-shaped spaces forms the transition to the development on the upper south side. The park area mediates between the small-scale development on the west side and the new.

Modell 1:500

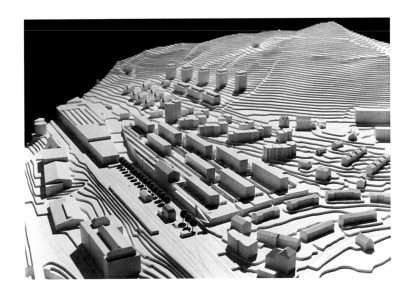

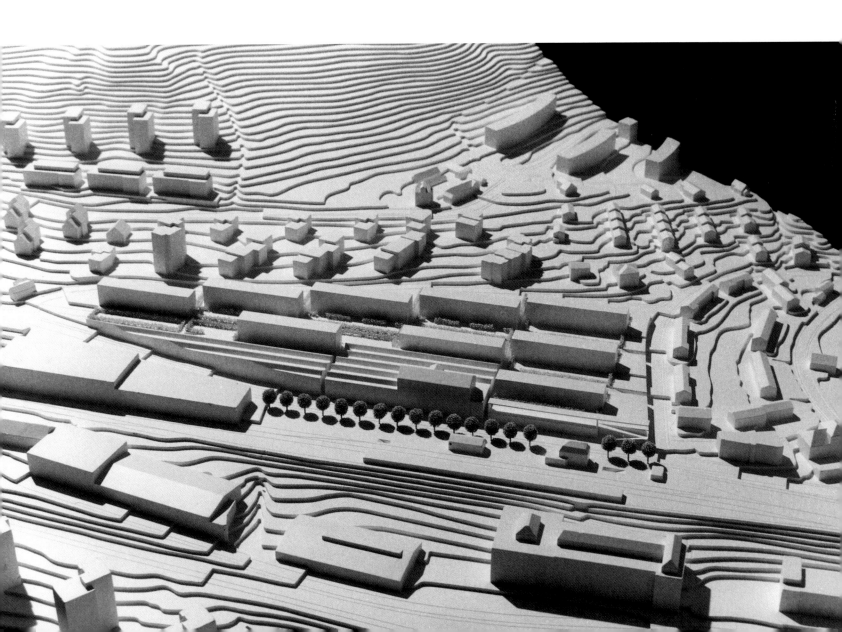

Before

After

N

Remarks ▮ Site size: approx. 118 000 square feet

REUTILIZATION OF THE TEXTILE INDUSTRY AREA KASTNER, THÜRINGEN, AUSTRIA, PROJECT 1990

Competition 1987, 1st prize ▮ Client: Municipality of Thüringen ▮ Collaborators: Crispin Amrein

The former textile factory, built between 1834 and 1837 by Scotsman John Douglas and co-financed by American Peter Kennedy and Swiss Alfred Escher, is reduced from five stories to three. The various additions that follow later on the west side of the ravine are reduced to the core buildings. A local museum will be placed in the one-story angular building and will open out toward the newly created, acutely angled outdoor space with a beautiful view of the valley. Five two-family homes, arranged in a fan-like shape, are located on the east side of the factory building. The detoured access from the village leads past these houses as a scenic pathway leading to the panorama terrace.

The unusual measure of the "story reduction," on the one hand, fulfills the wish for as many family apartments as possible on the first floor or the roof, with assigned outdoor spaces. On the other hand, the silhouette of the factory, which had been monumentalized by the earlier demolition of the ante-buildings, is somewhat fragmented by the reduction of the number of floors. Vertical light slits allow daylight to enter into the building volume.

Existing five-story factory ∎ Model 1:50

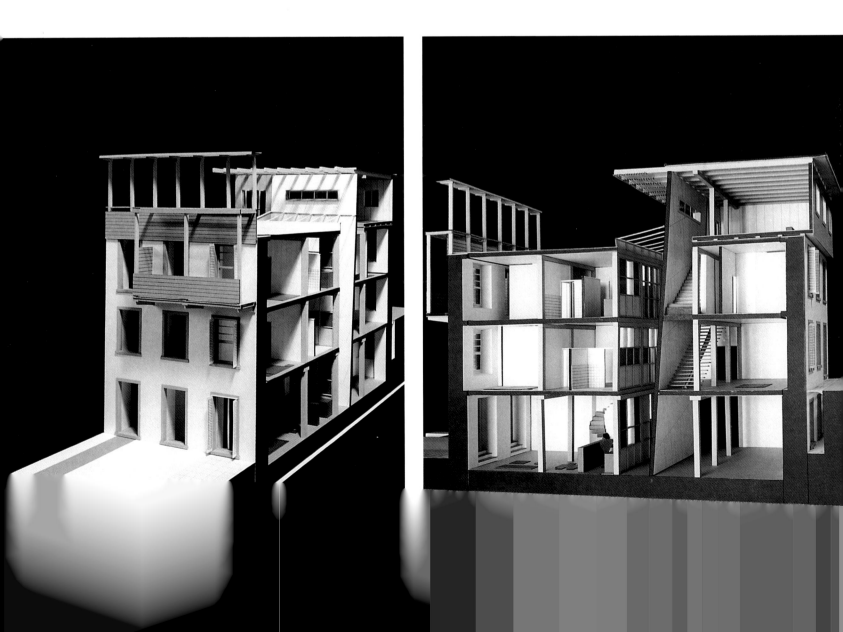

Before

After

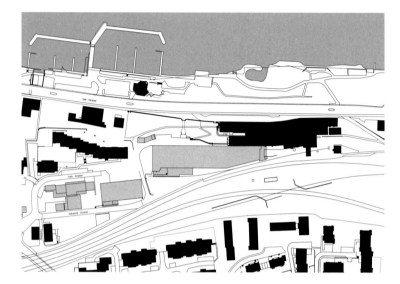

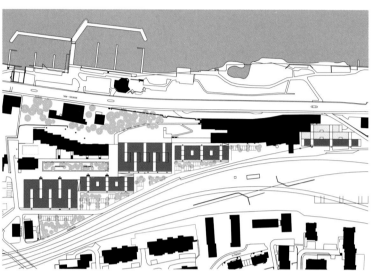

Remarks ▌ Site size: approx. 188 370 square feet ▌

Floors: 3 + 4 ▌ Use: 1.5

REUTILIZATION OF THE DYEWORKS INDUSTRIAL AREA WEIDMAN IN THALWIL, COMPETITION 1999

Project managment: Office Wuest & Partner, Martin Hofer, Zurich ▌ Client: Weidmann Management AG, Thalwil ▌

Collaborators: Barbara Ruppeiner, Claudia Murer, Andrea Calanchini ▌ Landscape architects: Kienast Vogt Partner, Zurich

In connection with the conversion of the area of the former dyeworks from an industrial zone into a modern services zone with a 33% share devoted to residential use, the halls between the edge of the slope and the railroad tracks are to be demolished and the grounds redeveloped. Most of the manufacturing buildings by the lake were demolished when the road along the lake was expanded. The halls on the slope, erected at a later date, will be preserved. Building volumes with a depth of eight, sixteen and thirty-two meters now occupy the plateau-like property. They form a sequence of autonomous building volumes with alternating silhouettes, comparable to the situation depicted in the 1894 engraving, with the longitudinally and transversely arranged shed halls. As is the case in the Thüringen project, daylight enters the interior through narrow light slits.

Old etching ▮ Model 1:100

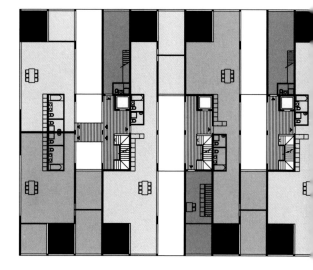

Ground plan apartment

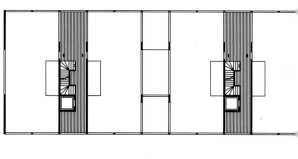

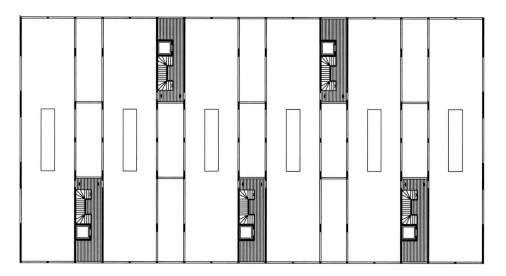

Ground plan offices 1:500

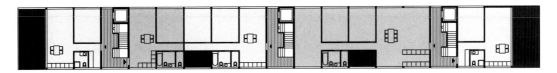

Ground plan apartment

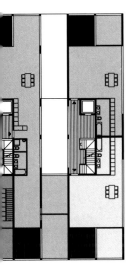

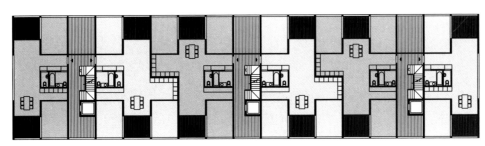

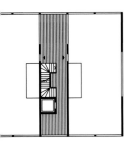

N

CONVERSION OF THE ERLA HOUSE, KAISERSTUHL, 1989

Client: Erla Immobilien, Laufenburg ▮ Collaborators: Crispin Amrein

The origins of the building – the basement – can be traced back with great certainty to the 13th or 14th century; the existing building substance dates back to the 17th century. The house is listed as a historic landmark. The floor-through entrance hall with the old staircase was preserved and renovated. A new service core, with the kitchen pushed up against it, serves to stabilize the house. On the first and second upper floors, a new hallway provides access to the rooms on the east side, which had been locked in. The large banquet hall on the third upper floor was restored in accordance with landmark preservation codes; the half-timbered construction was painted gray and set off with black shadow lines.

CONVERSION OF THE EGLOFF HOUSE, KAISERSTUHL, 1990

Client: Mr. and Mrs. Egloff, Kaiserstuhl ▮ Collaborators: Crispin Amrein

As in the case of the Erla House, the basement dates back to the 13th or 14th century and the majority of the existing building substance is from the 19th century. A new stairway and bathroom core develops the building and clarifies the ground plan typology. The new kitchens are located opposite the hallway and, at the same time, serve as entrance zones. A two-bedroom apartment with a separate entrance has been created on the first floor in the former Post restaurant. Both the third upper floor, a post-and-beam addition from a later period, and the attic floor have been developed as light-weight wood constructions.

Erla House (left) and Egloff House (right)

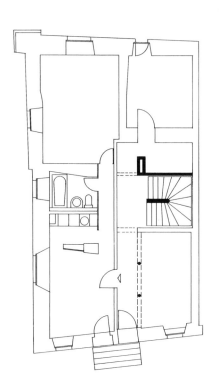
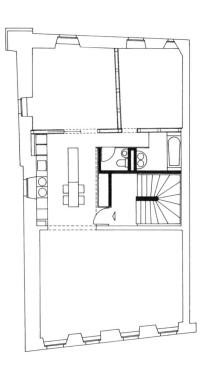
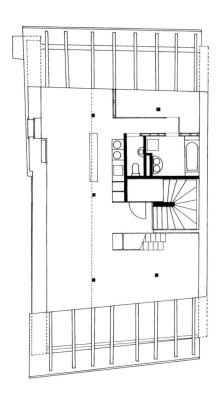

Egloff House: First floor   Upper floor   Attic floor 1:200

Egloff House: apartment entrance, kitchen ▌ Staircase

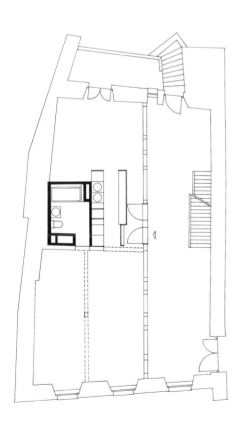
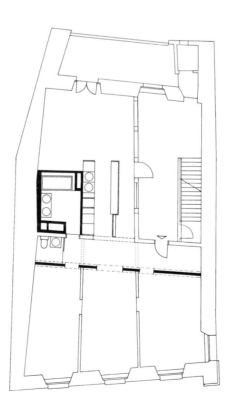
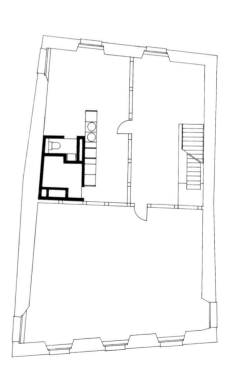

Erla House: Entrance floor   1st Upper floor   3rd Upper floor 1:200

Erla House: new corridor and open kitchen

BIOGRAPHIES

MARIANNE BURKHALTER, ARCHITECT BSA/SWB

	Raised in Thalwil
	Training as a structural engineering draftswoman
	in the office Hubacher and Issler, Zurich
1973–1975	student at Princeton University, USA
Since 1970	work as an architect in various offices and as a part-time
	freelancer. Stayed abroad for longer periods of time:
	1969–1972 Florence, Superstudio, 1970–1976 New York,
	Studio Works, 1977–1978 Los Angeles, Studio Works
1981–1983	Assistant with Professor Klaus Vogt at ETH Zurich
since 1984	Joint office with Christian Sumi in Zurich
1985	Assistant with Professor Mario Campi at ETH Zurich
1987	Guest professorship at Southern Institute of Architecture
	SCI-ARC in Los Angeles
1989	Birth of our son Luca-Andrea
1990–1997	Member of the urban image commission Baden
since 1998	Member of the building faculty of the city of Zurich
1999	Guest professorship at EPFL, Lausanne

CHRISTIAN SUMI, DIPL. ARCH. ETH/BSA/SIA

	Born in 1950 in Biel
	Studied architecture at ETH Zurich
1977	Diploma with Professor Dolf Schnebli
1978–1981	Collaboration with the German Archaeological
	Institute in Rome DAI
1980–1983	Scientific Assistant at the Institut gta
	at ETH Zurich (research: le Corbusier and
	the Immeuble Clarté in Geneva)
since 1984	Joint office with Marianne Burkhalter in Zurich
1989	Birth of our son Luca-Andrea
1989–1991	Diploma Assistant with Professor M. Campi, ETH Zurich
1990–1991	Guest professorship at the Ecole d'Architecture in Geneva
1994	Guest professorship in Harvard (Boston, USA)
1999	Guest professorship at EPFL, Lausanne

PRIZES AND AWARDS

Swiss Television "10 vor 10"/Hochparterre-Beste Architektur 1992: KV Schule, Laufenburg

Swiss Television "10 vor 10"/Hochparterre-Beste Architektur 1995: Hotel Zürichberg, Zurich

International Architectural Award "Bauen in den Alpen 1995": Forestry station Turbenthal

Minenergie 1998, Auszeichnung des Bundes: Redevelopment of the housing estate Dettenbühl, Wettswil

Thüringer Architectural Award 1998: Hotel Dorint, Weimar

EXHIBITIONS/FILMS

"Baukörper" Architektur Galerie 1991 in Luzern and Architektur Galerie Bonnier 1992 in Geneva

"Burkhalter und Sumi", ETH Zürich 1995, showed as a touring exhibition in: "Kulturzentrum de Singel" Antwerpen,

Architekturzentrum Wien, ETH Lausanne, Fachhochschule Trier, "Arc-en-rêve centre d'Architecture" Bordeaux

Holz: Alter Baustoff neu entdeckt, Video-Film Format NZZ, 1996

COLLABORATORS

Aeberhard Beat

Albertin Robert

Amrein Crispin

An Elaine

Åstrom Maria

Baer Nicole

Bassi Andrea

Beerli Yvonne

Bello Giorgio

Bergamelli Philipp

Bidom Martina

Bosshard Dani

Bradschaw Tomaso

Bräm Christine

Bucher Sibylle

Burkart Matthias

Büsser Roswitha

Carambellas Alexandra

Calanchini Andrea

Coderey Jeanne

Crivelli Marianne

Crola Angelika

Dutli Marianne

Dumont d'Ayot Catherine

Esposito Regula

Faust Stefan

Fingerhuth Lisina

Fischer Michael

Fischer Sabine

Froelich Adrian

Gabrijel Isabelle

Gantner Remo

Geschwentner Michael

Gijzen Marein

Gilbert Marc

Graham Mark

Gut Daniel

Hächler Gabi

Hecht Martin

Helland Bard

Hunziker Nadine

Imfeld Claudia

Item Urs

Kaiser Regula

Kiechle Monika

Klecak Lucie

Klostermann Rainer

Kohler Hermann

Koller Denise

Kopperschmidt Juliane

Kudva Neema

Lauener Donatus

Liechti Reto

Linsin Amade

Lubnow Volker

Mambourg Michèle

Mathey Dominique

Meneghelli Hamos

Michielin Filippo

Mileticki Maja

Morkowski Sabina

Murer Claudia

Nicol Michelle

Nigsch Sandra

Roth Andrea

Ruppeiner Barbara

Ruoss Silva

Rütsche Yvonne

Schmid Jürg

Schwendener Thomas

Sprenger Bernhard

Sunder-Plassmann Benedikt

Stotz Rainer

Turin Mireille

Vaszary Piroska

Walsh David

Wirth Toni

Wiskemann Barbara

Ziegler Pia

Ziegler Sybille

Marianne Burkhalter + Christian Sumi
Architects ETH/BSA/SIA/SWB

Münstergasse 18a
8001 Zürich
T +41 1 262 60 70
F +41 1 262 60 88
burkhaltersu@access.ch

BIBLIOGRAPHY

General

Texts

· Marianne Burkhalter und Christian Sumi:
"Ein Rückblick auf einen Ausblick – Fragen an Architekten"
in: Werk, Bauen + Wohnen, 9/89, p. 28–31

· Marianne Burkhalter und Christian Sumi: "Eugene Asse and
the Architectural Laboratory" in: Architectural Tests, Exhibition
catalog Architectural Gallery, Moscow 1997

· Marianne Burkhalter und Christian Sumi: "Forme et profession"
in: Pour une école de tendance mélanges offerts a Luigi Snozzi,
Presses polytechniques et unversitaires romandes,
Lausanne 1999, p. 64–66

Monographs

· Martin Steinmann: "Ein Ganzes aus Teilen, die ein Ganzes sind"
in: Marianne Burkhalter und Christian Sumi – Baukörper,
Edition Architekturgalerie Luzern, Luzern 1991, p. 17–22

· Martin Steinmann: "Planks between/on Uprights.
On the Architecture of Marianne Burkhalter and Christian Sumi"
in: Lotus international, 73/1992, p. 80–93 (engl. version
of "Ein Ganzes aus Teilen, die ein Ganzes sind")

· Martin Steinmann: "Sensuality and Sense"
in: a + u, no. 308, May 1996 p. 46/47

· Marcel Meili: "Über Gestalt und anderes"
in: Umbau, no. 13, November 1991

· Marcel Meili: "A propos de Forme et d'autre Chose"
in: Faces, no. 27, Spring 1993, p. 54–57
(french version of "Über Gestalt und anderes")

· "Marianne Burkhalter und Christian Sumi – Baukörper",
Edition Architekturgalerie Luzern, Luzern 1991

· Marianne Burkhalter und Christian Sumi – Die Holzbauten,
Institut gta Eidgenössische Technische Hochschule Zürich, 1995

· Marianne Burkhalter und Christian Sumi – De Houtbouw,
Institut gta Eidgenössische Technische Hochschule Zürich, 1995

· Marianne Burkhalter und Christian Sumi – The Timber Buildings,
Institut gta Eidgenössische Technische Hochschule Zürich, 1995

· "Marianne Burkhalter und Christian Sumi" in:
Architecture and Urbanism (a + u), no. 308, May 1996, p. 4–51

· "Marianne Burkhalter und Christian Sumi – Form and Profession" in:
AA Files, no. 34, Autumn 1997, p. 56–63

Swiss Architecture

· Peter Buchanan: "Swiss essentialists" in: The Architectural Review,
no. 1127, January 1/3 1991, p. 75/76

· Junta de Andalucía (Ed.): Architekten der deutschen Schweiz,
Sevilla 1992, p. 40–51

· Mark Gilbert, Kevin Alter (Ed.): Construction, Intention, Detail.
Zürich 1994, p. 32–39

· Kevin Alter: "Made in Switzerland. Formal concerns take a
back seat to experiential qualities in the work of four Swiss firms"
in: PA, Progressive Architecture, February 1995, p. 92–101 (p. 96/97)

· "Grado zero – Suizos del norte, una nueva simplicidad"
in: AV Arquitectura Viva, no. 41, March/April 1995, p. 50–53

· "Dossier Suisse Allemande" in: L'architecture d'aujourd'hui,
June 1995, no. 299, p. 84–89

· Ursula Suter: "Architekturszene Schweiz/Burkhalter & Sumi"
in: 5081 Architects in the World, Tokio 1995, p. 155

· "Architecture in Switzerland" in: Zlaty rez,
(Czech Republic) no. 10, summer 1995, p. 30–33

· "Barevné Svycarsko" in: Architekt (Czech Rebublic)
no. 25/26/1996, p. 24/25

· "Kindergarten Lustenau" in: Minimal Tradition. Max Bill
und die "einfache Architektur", Max Bill et l'architecture "simple"
1942–1996, XIX Triennale di Milano 1996, p. 104–107

· "Kindergarten Lustenau" in: Minimal Tradition. Max Bill e
l'architettura "semplice", Max Bill and "Simple" Architecture,
1942–1996, XIX Triennale di Milano 1996, p. 104–107

· Carmen Humbel-Schnurrenberger: "Naheliegendes als Provokation"
in: Facts, no. 37, 12. September 1996, p. 132/133

· "Arkitektur i Schweiz" in: Arkitektur, 5/1997, August, p. 36–43

· Ulrike Zophoniasson-Baierl: "Moderne: Längst Geschiche,
eine abgeschlossene Epoche" in: Basler Zeitung, Feuilleton,
October 8, 97, p. 41

· "Swiss German Architecture" in: SD Space Design 9802,
no. 401, February 1998, p. 10–13

· "A lagenbergi Allatkert éttermének atépitése" in: arc 1, Je pense
donc je suisse, Dominika Vamos (Ed.), Budapest 1998, p. 36–39

Architectural Guides/Dictionaries

· Beat Wyss (Ed.): Ars Helvetica XII. Die visuelle Kunst der Schweiz.
Kunstszenen heute, Disentis 1992, p. 271 (Haus Brunner)

· Pro Helvetia (Ed.): Frammenti, Interfacce, Intervalli.
Paradigmi della frammentazione nell'arte svizzera,
Genova 1992, p. 233 (Haus Brunner)

· Peter Disch (Ed.): Architektur in der deutschen Schweiz 1980–1990,
Lugano 1991, p. 209 (Haus Brunner), p. 211 (Hotel Zürichberg),
p. 232 (Haus Pircher + Häuser Egloff/Erla)

· Schweizer Architekturführer 1. Nordost- und Zentralschweiz
1920–1990, Zürich 1992, p. 124 (Haus Brunner)

· Schweizer Architekturführer 2. Nordwestschweiz, Jura, Mittelland
1920–1990, Zürich 1994, p. 112 (KV-Schule Laufenburg)

· Mercedes Daguerre: Guida all'architettura del Novecento, Svizzera,
Milano 1995, p. 20/114 (KV-Schule Laufenburg)

· Otto Kapfinger: "Ein Führer zu 260 sehenswerten Bauten"
in: Baukunst in Vorarlberg seit 1980, Ostfildern 1998, 3/11
(Kindergarten Lustenau)

· Christoph Allenspach: Architektur in der Schweiz – Bauen im
19. und 20. Jahrhundert, (Ed.) Pro Helvetia, Zürich 1998, p. 15, 151

· Architektur im 20. Jahrhundert – Schweiz, (Ed.) Anna Meseure,
Martin Tschanz und Wilfried Wang, Deutsches Architektur-Museum,
München 1998, p. 300–301 (Hotel Zürichberg)

· Isabelle Rucki und Dorothee Huber (Ed.): Architektenlexikon
der Schweiz, Basel 1998, p. 108

Wood

· Marianne Burkhalter und Christian Sumi – Die Holzbauten,
Institut gta Eidgenössische Technische Hochschule Zürich, 1995

· Pascale Joffroy: "Construction Bois en Suisse" in: Le Moniteur,
Architecture, no. 46, 11/1993, p. 42–48

· Catherine Seron-Pierre: "Construction en bois"
in: Le Moniteur, Architecture, no. 59, 3/1995, p. 46/47

· Benedikt Loderer: "Holz – eine Wiederentdeckung"
in: Passagen/Passages. Eine Schweizerische Kulturzeitschrift,
no. 20, Frühling 1996, p. 46/47

· Werner Blaser: Holz Pionier Architektur,
Weiningen-Zürich 1995, p. 170/171

· Naomi Stungo, The new Wood Architecture,
London 1998, p. 24–31, 56–65

Region

· Christoph Mayr-Fingerle (Ed.): Internationaler Architekturpreis
für neues Bauen in den Alpen, Basel 1996, p. 34–39

· Kunsthaus Bregenz (Ed.): Bau – Kultur – Region: Regionale Identität
im wachsenden Europa – das Fremde, Bregenz 1996

· Friedrich Achleitner: "Schweizer Architektur – aus östlicher Sicht"
(Eröffnungsrede der Ausstellung an der ETH Zürich, Januar 1995)
in: Region, ein Konstrukt? Regionalismus, eine Pleite?, Basel 1997

Technology

· "Architecture et Construction" Une discussion avec Kenneth Frampton, Marcel Meili, Bruno Reichlin, Wolfgang Schett, Christian Sumi in: Faces, no. 22, winter 1991, p. 18–25

· "Architektur und Konstruktion", (see above) german version in: Werk, Bauen + Wohnen, no. 11/12 1992

· Marianne Burkhalter und Christian Sumi: "Secciones comparadas" in: a + t, low tech – baja tecnologia, 9/1997, p. 126–135

· "Positive Indifferenz", Interview Lynnette Widder with Christian Sumi in: Daidalos, "Magie der Werkstoffe II", Special edition, August 1995, p. 26–34

Color

· Diego Peverelli: "Farbe als Komponente des architektonischen Konzepts" in: CRB Bulletin, 4/95, p. 12–15

· "Architektur und Farbe", Architektenkammer Berlin (Ed.), Berlin 1997, p. 24–29

· Steven Spier: "Red Shift" in: The Architectural Review, Colour, November 1998, p. 58–60

Housing

· AV Arquitectura Viva, Vievienda Mejor (Housing improved), no. 67, 1997, p. 12–17

· Bauwelt "In einer Reihe" no. 5, January 1997, p. 206–209

· Appartment Buildings, Architectural Design, Barcelona 1999, p. 30–39

Buildings and Projects by Burkhalter and Sumi

Haus Pircher, Eglisau, 1986

· Marianne Burkhalter: "Kleines Haus in Eglisau" in: archithese, 5/85, p. 25–27

· Verena Dietrich (Ed.): Architektinnen, Ideen – Projekte – Bauten, Stuttgart 1986, p. 52

· "Wohnhaus, als Stöckli genutzt, 8193 Eglisau/ZH" in: as Schweizer Architektur, no. 72, Mai 1986

· Marianne Burkhalter und Christian Sumi: "Due case di legno" in: Rivista Tecnica, 1–2/1988, p. 57–61

· Kay Wettstein: "Ein Holzhaus am Weinberg" in: Ideales Heim, 11/88, p. 123–130

· Inès Lamunière: "Un Visage de Zurich: ou de deux faces l'usage de panneau de coffrage. Projets récents de M. Burkhalter + Ch. Sumi et de Peter Märkli" in: Faces, no. 12, summer 1989, p. 24–36 (p. 30/31)

· Martin Steinmann: "Neue Architektur in der Schweiz" in: BauArt, 2/1990, p. 77

· "Wohnhaus Eglisau" in: Alfred Hablützel/Verena Huber: Innenarchitektur in der Schweiz 1942–1992, Vereinigung Schweizer Innenarchitekten (Ed.), Sulgen 1993, p. 234/235

· Martin Steinmann: "Planks between/on Uprights" in: Lotus international, 73/1992, p. 80–93

· "Haus Pircher" in: Marianne Burkhalter und Christian Sumi – Die Holzbauten, Institut gta Eidgenössische Technische Hochschule Zürich, 1995, p. 72–81

· Alfred Hablützel: Wege der Birke, Bern 1996

· Standardhäuser – Die Häuslbauer, Edited by Architektur Zentrum Wien, Wien 1997

Brunner House, Langnau am Albis, 1987

· Marianne Burkhalter und Christian Sumi: "Due case di legno" in: Rivista Tecnica, 1–2/1988, p. 57–61

· Marianne Burkhalter und Christian Sumi: "Una casa prefabbricata in legno" in: Casabella, no. 549, September 1988, p. 38

· Marianne Burkhalter und Christian Sumi: "Die Teile und das Ganze" in: Werk, Bauen + Wohnen, 9/89, p. 38–43

· Kay Wettstein: "Ein Holzhaus von elementarer Klarheit"
in: Ideales Heim, 2/1990, p. 18–25

· Pro Helvetia (Ed.): Frammenti, Interfacce, Intervalli. Paradigmi
della frammentazione nell'arte svizzera, Geneva 1992, p. 233

· Martin Steinmann: "Planks between/on Uprights"
in: Lotus international, 73/1992, p. 80–93

· "Haus Brunner" in: Marianne Burkhalter und Christian Sumi –
Die Holzbauten, Institut gta Eidgenössische Technische Hochschule
Zürich, 1995, p. 82–93

Street Installation, Biel 1986, in collaboration with
Christoph Haerle und Matthias Schaedler

· Ausstellungszeitung der 8. Schweizer Plastikausstellung Biel 1986,
1st edition p. 14, 2nd edition p. 13

· Andréa Meuli: "Kunst, die im Weg steht" in: du, 10/1986, p. 85–93

· Christian Sumi: "Eine prekäre Konstruktion"
in: Werk, Bauen + Wohnen, 11/90, p. 18–21

· Junta de Andalucía (Ed.): Architekten der deutschen Schweiz,
Sevilla 1992, p. 50

· "Strasseninstallation Biel 1986" in: Marianne Burkhalter
und Christian Sumi – Die Holzbauten, Institut gta Eidgenössische
Technische Hochschule Zürich, 1995, p. 40–47

Thüringen Development, Vorarlberg 1987

· Marianne Burkhalter und Christian Sumi: "Projekt Überbauung
ehemaliges Fabrikareal in Thüringen, Vorarlberg" in: Liechtensteiner
Almanach, 1989, p. 223/224

Quarter Center Schwamendingen in Zürich, 1988/1998

· Othmar Humm: "Quartierzentrum für Schwamendingen"
in: Bau + Architektur, 12/1988, p. 29–32

· Benedikt Loderer: "Das einfache Bauen öffentlich"
in: Hochparterre, no. 12, 1988, p. 14/15

· Inès Lamunière: "Un visage de Zurich: ou de deux faces l'usage de
panneau de coffrage. Projets récents de M. Burkhalter + Ch. Sumi et
de Peter Märkli" in: Faces, no. 12, summer 1989, p. 24–36 (p. 26/27)

· Martin Steinmann: "Planks between/on Uprights"
in: Lotus international, 73/1992, p. 80–93

Egloff House, Kaiserstuhl, 1990
Erla House, Kaiserstuhl, 1989

· Heinrich Helfenstein: "Transformation des maisons Egloff et Erla
à Kaiserstuhl, 1989/90" in: Faces, no. 23, spring 1992, p. 12/13

· Heinrich Helfenstein: "Marianne Burkhalter, Christian Sumi.
Due interni a Kaiserstuhl" in: Domus, no. 740, July/August 1992,
p. 50–55

· Martin Steinmann: "Planks between/on Uprights"
in: Lotus international, 73/1992, p. 80–93

· "House Egloff and House Erla" in: SD Space Design,
26/1995, p. 118–121

Competition Röntgenstrasse, Zurich, 1990

· Matteo Brändli: "Marianne Burkhalter e Christian Sumi dal tracciato
alla rampa" in: Casabella, no. 600, April 1993, p. 22/23

Triemli Hospital Zürich, 1991

· Martin Tschanz: "Entwerfen mit Industrieprodukten: Pathos
und Pragmatismus" in: archithese, 5/93, p. 32–45

· Marianne Burkhalter and Christian Sumi:
"Triemli Spital. Nuevas fachadas" in: Quaderns, no. 201, 1993,
special edition "Renovating", p. 96–101

· Gilles Barbey: "Spurensicherung als kulturelle Aufgabe"
in: Werk, Bauen + Wohnen, 12/1993, p. 6–22 (p.18/19)

· "Baukörper" Ausstellung in der Architekturgalerie Luzern, 1991
und der Galerie Bonnier in Genf 1993
· Roman Hollenstein: "Ein vielversprechendes Architektenteam"
in: NZZ, Planen – Bauen – Wohnen, 18.10.91, p. 67
· Roman Hollenstein: "Sucht nach dem Konkreten" in: NZZ, Feuilleton,
19.03.93, p. 27

Composting Plant Werdhölzli, Zurich, 1992
· Marianne Burkhalter und Christian Sumi:
"Kompostieranlage Werdhölzli, Zürich Altstetten, Projekt 1993"
in: Werk, Bauen + Wohnen, 9/1993, p. 6–30
· Marianne Burkhalter und Christian Sumi: "Kompostieranlage
Werdhölzli/Zürich" in: Bauwelt, 1/2, January 1995, p. 48/49

Business School, Laufenburg,1992
· Benedikt Loderer: "Kein eindeutiges Objekt"
in: Hochparterre, 11/1992, p. 52
· "Kaufmännische Schule Laufenburg, 1992"
in: Werk, Bauen + Wohnen 12/1992, p. 14–19
· Martin Steinmann: "Planks between/on Uprights"
in: Lotus international, 73/1992, p. 80–93
· Junta de Andalucía (Ed.): "Architekten der
deutschen Schweiz", Sevilla 1992, p. 42–46
· Otti Gmür: "Rundgang durch ein Schulhaus"
in: Kunst und Kirche, 3/93, p. 14–19
· "Ecole de Laufenburg" in: Faces no. 27, spring 1993, p. 54–57
· Carmen Humbel: "Burkhalter e Sumi. Edificio scolastico a
Laufenburg/Aarau" in: Domus, no. 754, November 1993, p. 18/19
· Pascale Joffroy: "Construction Bois en Suisse" in: Le Moniteur,
Architecture, no. 46, 11/1993, p. 45

· Matthias Ackermann: "Die Stadt und ihre Schule" in: NZZ,
Planen – Bauen – Wohnen, March 5, 93, p. 67
· Marianne Burkhalter und Christian Sumi: "Farbe und Betonung
von Raum und Körper" in: archithese, 6/94, p. 48/49
· "Ecole à Laufenburg, Suisse" in: Séquences Bois,
Les bâtiments éducatifs, September 1994, p. 10
· "Ecole à Laufenburg" in: l'architecture d'aujourd'hui,
June 1995, no. 299, p. 85
· "Commercial School, Laufenburg"
in: a + u, no. 308, May 1996, p. 20–27
· "Business School" in: AA Files, no. 34, 1997, p. 57
· Steven Spier: "School boards" in: The Architectural Review,
no. 1199, January 1997, p.46/47
· "Skola, Laufenburg" in: Arkitektur, 5/1997, August, p. 40/41
· "Kaufmännische Schule Laufenburg, 1992" in: Architektur
und Farbe, 1997, p. 24–27

Forestry Station Turbenthal, 1993
· Pascale Joffroy: "Construction Bois en Suisse"
in: Le Moniteur, Architecture, no. 46, 11/1993, p. 44
· Marianne Burkhalter e Christian Sumi. Strutture
per le guardie forestali nei boschi intorno. a Zurigo"
in: Domus, no. 763, 9/94, p. 32–35
· Marianne Burkhalter und Christian Sumi: "Forstwerkhof Turbenthal"
in: Holz Bulletin, 37/1994, Umhüllen, Bl. 530/31
· "Forstwerkhof in Turbenthal" in: Mark Gilbert, Kevin Alter (Ed.):
Construction, Intention, Detail. Fünf Projekte von fünf Schweizer
Architekten, Zürich 1994, p. 32–39
· Marianne Burkhalter und Christian Sumi: "Standardisierte
Forstwerkhöfe" in: Werk, Bauen + Wohnen, 5/1994, p. 40–44
· Marianne Burkhalter und Christian Sumi: "Forstwerkhof Turbenthal"
in: du, Die Zeitschrift der Kultur, no. 11, November 1994

· Marianne Burkhalter und Christian Sumi:
"Forstwerkhof in Turbenthal/Forestry Station in Turbenthal"
in: Detail, no. 3, 1995, p. 440–445

· Kevin Alter: "Made in Switzerland. Formal concerns take a back
seat to experiential qualities in the work of four Swiss firms" in:
PA, Progressive Architecture, February 1995, p. 92–101 (p. 96/97)

· Marianne Burkhalter und Christian Sumi: "Forstwerkhof Turbenthal"
in: Bauwelt 17, May 1995, 86. Jahrgang, p. 974/975

· "Architecture in Switzerland" in: Zlaty rez, (Czech Republic)
no. 10, summer 1995, p. 30–33

· Werner Blaser: "Holz Pionier Architektur", 1995, p. 170/171

· "Forstwerkhof Turbenthal" in: Marianne Burkhalter
und Christian Sumi – Die Holzbauten, Institut gta Eidgenössische
Technische Hochschule Zürich, 1995, p. 48–61

· Christoph Mayr-Fingerle (Ed.): Internationaler Architekturpreis
für neues Bauen in den Alpen, Basel 1996, p. 34–39

· "Two Standardized Forestry Stations"
in: a + u, no. 308, May 1996, p. 6–19

· Kunsthaus Bregenz, (Ed.): "Bau – Kultur – Region: Regionale Identität
im wachsenden Europa – das Fremde", Bregenz 1996, p. 80–87

· "Two Forestry Stations" in: AA Files, no. 34, 1997, p. 58

· "Forestry Station in Turbenthal" in: Naomi Stungo,
The new Wood Architecture, London 1998, p. 56–61

Forestry Station Rheinau, 1994

· Marianne Burkhalter und Christian Sumi: "Standardisierte
Forstwerkhöfe" in: Werk, Bauen + Wohnen, 5/1994, p. 40–44

· "Marianne Burkhalter e Christian Sumi.
Strutture per le guardie forestali nei boschi intorno a Zurigo"
in: Domus, no. 763, 9/94, p. 32–35

· Marianne Burkhalter und Christian Sumi: "Prototipo natural.
Estacion de trabajos forestales, Rheinau, Zurich" in: Arquitectura
Viva, no. 41, March/April 1995, p. 50–53

· Marianne Burkhalter und Christian Sumi: "Casas forestales
Rheinau/Forestry huts" in: a + t, no. 5, April 1995, p. 8–20

· "Standardizirované hájovny/standardized Gamekeeper's Lodges"
in: Zlaty rez/golden section, no. 10, summer 1995, p. 30–33

· "Abri Forestier à Rheinau" in: l'architecture d'aujourd'hui,
June 1995, no. 299, p. 86/87

· "Forstwerkhof Rheinau" in: Marianne Burkhalter und
Christian Sumi – Die Holzbauten, Institut gta Eidgenössische
Technische Hochschule Zürich, 1995, p. 62–71

· "Two Standardized Forestry Stations" in: (a + u),
no. 308, May 1996, p. 6–19

· Kunsthaus Bregenz (Ed.): "Bau – Kultur – Region: Regionale Identität
im wachsenden Europa – das Fremde", Bregenz 1996, p. 80-87

· "Two Forestry Stations" in: AA Files, no. 34, 1997, p. 58

· "Forestry Station in Rheinau" in: Naomi Stungo,
The new Wood Architecture, London 1998, p. 62–65

Kindergarten am Schlatt, Lustenau, Austria, 1994

· Bruno Reichlin: "Une légèreté du Jouet. Jardin d'enfants,
Lustenau, architectes Marianne Burkhalter et Christian Sumi"
in: Faces, no. 33, 1994, p. 21–23

· Fabrizio Gellera: "Architectura nel Canton Zurigo" in:
Rivista Tecnica, 11/94, p. 34–36

· Ursina Jakob: "Formvollendung oder Nutzungsqualität" in:
NZZ, Planen – Bauen – Wohnen, June 3, 1994, p. 71

· "Kindergarten "Am Schlatt" Lustenau, Vorarlberg" in: Wettbewerbe,
Heft 139/140, 19. Jahrgang, Jan./Febr. 1995, p. 127–131

· Catherine Seron-Pierre: "Construction en bois" in: Le Moniteur,
Architecture, no. 59, 3/1995, p. 46/47

· Marianne Burkhalter und Christian Sumi: "Jardin de infancia
en Lustenau/Kindergarden" in: a + t, no. 5, April 1995, p. 20–23

· "Jardin d'Enfants à Lustenau" in: l'architecture d'aujourd'hui,
June 1995, no. 299, p. 88/89

· "Kindergarten am Schlatt" in: Marianne Burkhalter und
Christian Sumi – Die Holzbauten, Institut gta Eidgenössische
Technische Hochschule Zürich, 1995, p. 94–111

· Karin Gimmi: "Kindergarten Lustenau" in: Minimal Tradition. Max Bill
und die "einfache Architektur" 1942–1996, XIX Triennale
di Milano 1996, Bundesamt für Kultur (Ed.), Baden 1996, p. 104–107

· Alfred Hablützel: Wege der Birke, 1996

· "Kindergarten am Schlatt" in: a + u, no. 308, May 1996, p. 28–35

· "Kindergarten" in: AA Files, no. 34, 1997, p. 59

· Steven Spier: "Red Shift" in: The Architectural Review,
November 1998, p. 58–60

· "Kindergarten Lustenau" in: Architectural Magazine B
(Dänemark) no. 54, 1998

· "Kindergarten Lustenau" in: Naomi Stungo, The new Wood
Architecture, London. 1998, p. 24–31

Hotel Zürichberg, Zurich, 1995

· Junta de Andalucía (Ed.): Architekten der deutschen Schweiz,
Sevilla 1992, p. 47–49

· Matteo Brändli: "Marianne Burkhalter e Christian Sumi dal
tracciato alla rampa" in: Casabella no. 600, April 1993, p. 22/23

· Marianne Burkhalter und Christian Sumi:
"Erweiterungsbau Hotel Zürichberg, Zürich, Projekt 1993"
in: Werk, Bauen + Wohnen, 9/1993, p. 20

· Köbi Gantenbein: "Das Oval und das Denkmal"
in: Hochparterre, no. 10, 1993, p. 35

· Roman Hollenstein: "Der Pavillon im Park – ein architektonisches
Juwel" in: NZZ, 12. April 1995, p. 53

· Benedikt Loderer: "Hotel Zürichberg" in: Hochparterre,
no. 6/7, 1995, p. 18–25

· Friedrich Achleitner: "Marianne Burkhalter und Christian Sumi.
Das Modell vom Zürichberg" in: Architektur aktuell, no. 183,
September 1995, p. 46–55

· Friedrich Achleitner: "Renovation – Invention", Heinrich Helfenstein:
"Images du sol", Dieter Kienast, Günther Vogt: "Perception et Projet
de Paysage" in: Faces no. 39, Automn 1996, p. 64–69

· Marianne Burkhalter und Christian Sumi: "Neubau
Hotel Zürichberg" in: Werk, Bauen + Wohnen, 12/1995, p. 26–31

· Regula Michel: "Ein Temperenzhotel auf dem Zürichberg"
in: Zürcher Denkmalpflege, 1995/96, p. 74–86

· "Renovation and Extension of Hotel Zürichberg"
in: a + u, no. 308, May 1996, p. 36–43

· Marianne Burkhalter und Christian Sumi:
"Extension en spirale – Hôtel Zürichberg" in: créé. architecture
intérieure, no. 270, 1996, p. 74–79

· "Barevné Svycarsko" in: Architekt (Czech Republic)
no. 25–26/1996, p. 24/25

· Lynnette Widder: "Hotel Zürichberg" in: Daidalos,
"Übernachten – Sleeping out", no. 62, Dezember 1996, p. 98–103

· Philipp Meuser: "Hotel – Oval mit Parkhaus – Schleife" in:
Bauwelt, no. 4, January 1996, p. 144–149

· Steven Spier: "Swiss roll" in: The Architectural Review,
no. 1199, January 1997, p. 42–45

· "Extension d'un monument historique" in: Séquences Bois,
Hébergement et restauration, December 1997, p. 8–11

· "Renovation and extension of Hotel Zürichberg" in:
AA Files, no. 34, 1997, p. 60/61

· *"Renovering och Tillbyggnad av Hotel Zürichberg, Zürich"*

in: Arkitektur, 5/1997, August, p. 36–39

· M. Gyöngy Katalin: *"Térspiràl, A Zürichberg Szàlloda Bövitése"*

in: Epités Felujitas, 5. Szam July/August 1997, p. 34–39

· *"Hotel Zürichberg, Zürich"* in: Architektur und Farbe, 1997, p. 28/29

· *"Stimmungen"* in: 20 Jahre Architektur & Technik, 1998, p. 161

· *"Hotel Zürichberg, Zurich"* in: SD Space Design 9802,

no. 401, February 1998, p. 10–13

· *"Hotel Zürichberg"* in: Otto Riewoldt, Hotel Design,

London 1998, p. 120–123

· *"Hotel Zürichberg"* in: Oliver de Vleeschouwerts, New Hotel

Designs, Hôtel étonnants (French edition), Aussergewöhnliche

Hotels (German edition), Paris 1999, p. 102–107

"Marianne Burkhalter und Christian Sumi",
Touring Exhibition of ETH Zürich 1995

· Philipp Meuser: *"Die Wahrnehmung des Raumes"*

in: NZZ, 15. January 1996, p. 25

Cooperative Apartments WGL, Laufenburg, 1996

· *"Wohnbau in Laufenburg"* in: Architektur aktuell,

Oktober 1996, p. 54–65

· *"Casa d'apparamenti a Laufenburg"* in: Domus, no. 791,

March 1997, p. 33–37

· *"Bostadshus, Laufenburg"* in: Arkitektur, 5/1997, August, p. 42/43

· *"Addition farbiger Kuben"* in: Bauwelt, no. 5, Januar 1997,

p. 206–209

· *"Bloque de viviendas, Laufenburg, Suiza"* in: AV Arquitectura Viva,

no. 67, 1997, p. 12–17

· *"Block of flats on the Heimweg"* in: AA Files, no. 34, 1997, p. 62/63

· *"WGL Laufenburg"* in: Appartment Buildings, Architectural Design,

Barcelona 1999, p. 30–39

· *"Ai margini del centro storico di Laufenburg, un gioioso intervento

residenziale"* in: Housing, no. 9, November 1998, p. 38/39

Redevelopment Dettenbühl, Wettswil, 1996

· Marianne Burkhalter und Christian Sumi:

"Sanierung Wohnsiedlung Dettenbühl, Wettswil, 1996"

in: Werk, Bauen + Wohnen, no. 6, June 1997, p. 16–23

· *"Wohnsiedlung Dettenbühl, Wettswil-Zürich"* in: Gebäudesanierung

nach Minergie-Standard, (Ed.) Energiefachstellen der Kantone Bern,

Zürich, Thurgau und Neuchâtel, Zürich 1998, p. 28–31

· Silvia Huber: *"Minergie im Aufwind"* in: Architektur + Technik, 8/99

Development Hechlenberg, Herrliberg, 1996

· Catherine Séron-Pierre: *"maison pour quatre familles"*

in: Le Moniteur, Architecture, no. 81, June 1997, p. 54/55

Development Melchrüti, Wallisellen, 1997

· Andres Janser: *"Variierter Typ"* in: archithese, no. 1, 1998, p. 46–51

Hotel Dorint, Weimar, Germany, 1997

· Gerd Zimmermann und Jörg Brauns: *"Beethovenplatz/Dorint-

Hotel"* in: KulturStadtBauen, Eine architektonische Wanderung

durch Weimar – Kulturstadt Europas , 1997, p. 86–89

· Gerd Zimmermann: *"Die Ordnung des Domizils,

das neue Dorint Hotel in Weimar"* in: Weimar Kultur Journal,

no. 2/1999, p. 12–14

· Oliver G. Hamm: *"Ein später Triumph der Moderne"*

in: NZZ, 7.4.99, Feuilleton p. 65

· Reinhard Seiss: *"Stadtkultur versus Kulturstadt"*

in: Architektur Aktuell, no. 227 April 1999, p. 111

· *Eva Maria Froschauer: "Spannungsfeld Buchenwald*

und Goethe Haus" in: archithese, *no. 2, 1999, p. 20*

Wood Pavilion Game Park Langenberg, Langnau am Albis, 1998

· *"A lagenbergi Allatkert éttermének atépitése" in:* arc 1, Je pense

donc je suisse, Dominika Vamos (Ed.), Budapest 1998, p. 36–39

Dome Interior/Visualization Center, ETH Zurich, 1997

· *Roderick Hönig: Der Visualisierungstempel"*

in: NZZ, *26.March 1999, p. 47*

· *Kaye Geipel: "Vorhang auf – Kuppelausbau der ETH Zürich"*

in: Bauwelt, *no. 7, February 99, p. 322/323*

Condensed Housing Berlin-Köpenick 1998

· *"Das städtische Haus", Dokumentation der Wettbewerbs-*

ergebnisse, Senatsverwaltung für Bauen, Wohnen und Verkehr (Ed.),

Berlin 1998, p. 52–53

Redevelopment EMPA, Dübendorf, 1999

· *Peter Omachen: "Ökonomie der Mittel" in:* archithese,

no. 2, 1998, p. 22/23

Publications by Marianne Burkhalter
General

· *Marianne Burkhalter, Michael Koch, Claude Lichtenstein,*

Tomaso Zanoni: "Freudenberg – der Architekt Jacques Schader und

die Kantonsschule in Zürich-Enge, (Ed.) Museum für Gestaltung

Zürich und Schweizerischer Werkbund, Zürich 1992

Buildings and Projects

Community Centers in Columbus Ohio

(Collaboration Studio Works in New York), 1971

· *"Centro sociale for a community"*, Domus, *no. 548/1975, p. 33*

· *R. Mangurian and Craig Hodgetts: "South Side Settlement",*

Columbus Ohio, 1978–1980

· *John Morris Dixon: "Memory materialized.*

South Side Settlement, Columbus, Oh.", Mark Mack: "Critique"

in: PA, Progressive Architecture, *2/1981, p. 78–85*

· *"CDA: Dialogue Continues" in:* South Side Express,

Volume 6, no. 7, November 1979

· *"Excavation: South Side Columbus" in:* Skyline May, *1980, p. 14/15*

Development railroad station in Luzern, Apartment and Office Build-

ings Inseli-quai and Reception Building, competition, 1st Prize,

in collaboration with Amman und Baumann in Luzern, 1977–1980

· archithese *3/85*

· *Otti Gmür: "3 Aktuelle Städtecollagen. Luzern: Bahnhof"*

in: Werk/Archithese *33/34, 1979, p. 40–50*

Publications by Christian Sumi
General

· *"Rancate" in:* Aldo Rossi, Eraldo Consolascio, Max Bosshard.

La Construzione del Territorio nel Cantone Ticino, Fondazione Ticino

Nostro, Venezia 1976, p. 495–504

· *Bauten von O.R. Salvisberg in Bern: im Bund 1977*

· *Together with Jürg Reber: Das Bieler Volkshaus*

in: Werk/Archithese, *23–24/78*

· *"Spitalbauten" und "Detailzeichnungen" (together with*

Ernst Strebel) in: O.R. Salvisberg – die andere Moderne, Zürich 1985,

p. 196–205 and p. 206–217

· "Holzhausbau heute" in: Konrad Wachsmann. Holzhausbau,
Basel 1995
· "Building the Wooden House Today" in: Konrad Wachsmann,
Building the Wooden House, Basel 1995 (English edition)
· Christian Sumi together with Regina Böhm, Daniela Däumler and
Tobias Haag: " Konrad Wachsmann: Architekt und Pionier des Indus-
triellen Bauens in: Konservierung der Moderne? Icomos, Heft des
Deutschen Nationalkomitees no. 24, München 1998, p. 56–62

About Le Corbusier
· "Il Progetto Wanner" in: Rassegna, 3/80
· "Vom Mehrfamilienhaus konzipiert als Villas Superposées
zum Mehrfamilienhaus als kollektives Wohnhaus" in:
Le Corbusier – La Ricerca paziente, Lugano 1980
· "L'immeuble Clarté et la conception de la maison à sec"
in: Le Corbusier à Genève 1922–32, Lausanne 1987
· "Clarté (immeuble)" and "Wanner (Edmond)"
in: Le Corbusier, une encyclopédie, monographie,
Centre Georges Pompidou, Paris 1987
· "Das Treppenhaus der Immeuble Clarté in Genf, 1932, von
Le Corbusier und Pierre Jeanneret" in: Werk, Bauen + Wohnen, 6/89
· "Immeuble Clarté" in: Sulle tracce di Le Corbusier,
Venezia 1989, p. 176–187
· "The immeuble Clarté" in: The footsteps of Le Corbusier,
New York 1991, p. 176–187
· Christian Sumi, "Immeuble Clarté Genf 1932
von Le Corbusier und Pierre Jeanneret – Immeuble villa/
plan libre/maison à sec", Zürich 1989

Collaboration in Exhibitions
· Le Corbusier: "La ricerca pazienta", Lugano, 1980
· O. R. Salvisberg – "Die andere Moderne", 1985
· "Le Corbusier à Genève", 1987
· "L'aventure Le Corbusier", Paris, Centre Georges Pompidou, 1987

Buildings and Projects
Competition in three phases, Luzern station,
together with Marie-Claude Bétrix, Eraldo Consolascio,
Patrick Huber, Bruno Reichlin, 1976–79
· Aktuelle Wettbewerbsszene 5/76
· Diego Peverelli: "Ideenwettbewerb
Bahnhofgebiet Luzern" in: Werk/Archithese, 2/1977, p. 20–28
· Otti Gmür: "Luzern: Bahnhof" in: Werk/Archithese, 33–34/1979,
p. 40–50

Competition Papierareal in Zürich, together with
Heinrich Helfenstein and Margareta Peters, 1979
· Mario Botta: "Progetti per la città, progetti contro la città" in: Lotus
international, 25/79, p. 108–118
· "Der Wettbewerb für die Überbauung des Papierareals in Zürich"
in: Werk, Bauen + Wohnen, 6/1980, p. 29–47

Project for the Archeological Museum
in Metaponto (South of Italy), 1981
· Christian Sumi: "Museum. Projekt für ein archäologisches Museum
in Süditalien (Metaponto) 1980/81" in: Werk, Bauen + Wohnen,
4/1982, p. 4–5
· Christian Sumi: "Museo a Metaponto (1982)"
in: Parametro, no. 121, Nov/83, p. 58

Project Lässer House near Biel,
together with Margareta Peters, 1982
· Christian Sumi + Margareta Peters: "Entwurf eines Hauses bei Biel"
in: archithese, 1/84, p. 9–11

SHORT BIOGRAPHIES

Heinrich Helfenstein – *architectural photographer, lives and works in Zurich.*

Lynnette Widder – *architect, lives in New York and teaches at Rhode Island School of Design.*

Steven Spier – *architect, lives in London and teaches at South Bank University London.*

Eugene Asse – *architect, lives in Moscow and teaches at the Moscow Institute for Architecture.*

Detlef Mertins – *architect, lives in Toronto and teaches at Toronto University .*

THANKS

We would like to thank the following people for their assistance with this book: Isabelle Rucki for establishing the first contact with Birkhäuser Publishers; those responsible at Birkhäuser Publishers for their patience; Heinrich Helfenstein who has been accompanying our work photographically for over 10 years, for the extensive picture material; Lynnette Widder, Eugene Asse, Detlef Mertins, Steven Spier for their exciting texts; the office Kienast Vogt Partner – landscape architects in Zurich with who we've been collaborating for years for the special plan material; finally, the various clients for their permission to publish the plan materials as well as Claudia Murer and Andrea Roth for going through the plans in our office.

ENGLISH TRANSLATION
Katja Steiner and Bruce Almberg, Ehingen
(Spier, Asse, and Mertins essays)
Joseph Imorde, Zurich (Widder essay)

GRAPHIC DESIGN
Karin Weisener, Birkhäuser –
Publishers for Architecture

PHOTO CREDITS
Municipal Archives Zurich p. 49
Claus Bach, Weimar p. 43/47
Heinz Unger, Zurich p. 38/39/40/41
Burkhalter + Sumi, Zurich p. 181 top
All other photographs by
Heinrich Helfenstein, Zurich

© 1999 Birkhäuser – Publishers for Architecture
P.O. Box 133, CH-4010 Basel, Switzerland
Printed on acid-free paper
produced of chlorine-free pulp. TCF ∞
Printed in Italy

ISBN 1-56898-186-4
Licence edition published in North America
by Princeton Architectural Press
Princeton Architectural Press
37 East 7th Street New York, NY 10003
www.papress.com

ISBN 3-7643-5929-3
Published outside North America
by Birkhäuser Publishers
Birkhäuser – Publishers for Architecture,
P.O. Box 133, CH-4010 Basel, Switzerland
www.birkhauser.ch

(This book is also available in German, ISBN 3-7643-5928-5)

9 8 7 6 5 4 3 2 1

A CIP catalogue record for this book is available
from the Library of Congress, Washington D. C., USA

Die Deutsche Bibliothek – CIP-Einheitsaufnahme

Marianne Burkhalter + Christian Sumi.
-Basel ; Boston ; Berlin : Birkhäuser, 1999
Dt. Ausgabe. u.d.T.: Marianne Burkhalter + Christian Sumi
ISBN 3-7643-5929-3